SERVING ELIZABETH

Serving Elizabeth

Marcia Johnson

Serving Elizabeth
first published 2020 by Scirocco Drama
An imprint of J. Gordon Shillingford Publishing Inc.
© 2020 Marcia Johnson

Scirocco Drama Editor: Glenda MacFarlane

Cover design by Doowah Design
Author photo by Joanna Haughton
Cover illustration by Jennifer Taylor Paravantes
Production Photos by Barbara Zimonick

Printed and bound in Canada on 100% post-consumer recycled paper.
We acknowledge the financial support of the Manitoba Arts Council and
The Canada Council for the Arts for our publishing program.

Production inquiries to:
Colin Rivers, Managing Literary Agent
Marquis Entertainment Inc.
73 Richmond St West, Suite #312,
Toronto, ON M5H 4E8
416-960-9123 x 223
info@mqlit.ca

Library and Archives Canada Cataloguing in Publication

Title: Serving Elizabeth / Marcia Johnson.
Names: Johnson, Marcia, author.
Description: A play.
Identifiers: Canadiana 20200266624 | ISBN 9781927922620 (softcover)
Classification: LCC PS8619.O468 S47 2020 | DDC C812/.6—dc23

J. Gordon Shillingford Publishing
P.O. Box 86, RPO Corydon Avenue, Winnipeg, MB Canada R3M 3S3

For Cynthia Johnson.

Marcia Johnson

Marcia Johnson's plays include *Binti's Journey*, an adaptation of *The Heaven Shop* by Deborah Ellis (Theatre Direct Canada/ Manitoba Theatre for Young People/Black Theatre Workshop); *Courting Johanna* (Blyth Festival) based on Alice Munro's "Hateship, Friendship, Courtship, Loveship, Marriage," and *Late* (Obsidian Theatre Company).

My Mother's Ring, for which she wrote the libretto with composer Stephen A. Taylor, was nominated for a 2009 Dora Mavor Moore Award. Their second collaboration, *Paradises Lost*, based on the Ursula K. Le Guin novella, had excerpted concert performances by Third Angle Ensemble in Portland, Oregon and at The Gershwin Hotel in New York. It had its premiere at University of Illinois and a concert performance at Musical Works in Concert during the SummerWorks Festival.

Marcia is a core member of Got Your Back Canada and is a juror/dramaturg for Ergo Pink Fest, supporting, developing and showcasing the works of women and playwrights of marginalized genders.

Playwright's Notes

Many people who read or see *Serving Elizabeth* will know which streaming series inspired its creation. The series was extremely well-made and, at this moment (April 2020), I have seen every single episode. But a particular episode, the one set in Kenya, still stands out as flawed to me. The Kenyan perspective was completely ignored. I did not know what to do with my disappointment and frustration.

Fortunately, the next day, I learned that Thousand Islands Playhouse (TIP) had put out a call for its 2017 playwrights' unit. The theatre, in honour of Canada's one hundred and fifty years of confederation, was looking to help develop plays that reflected on colonialism. I wrote my proposal for *Heavy is the Head* (*Serving Elizabeth*'s original title) in less than thirty minutes and sent it off. I got selected for the group and proceeded to vent my spleen; writing the first draft in eight months in time for the Sneak Peek readings for TIP's loyal audience. I wrote this play to give voice to the underrepresented and was nervous about how it would be received. I was thrilled that the themes and characters resonated with those gathered.

I'm deeply indebted to Alexis Diamond for encouraging me to apply for the Playwrights Unit and everyone at TIP who read and gave feedback, including Carolyn Bennett, Brett Christopher, Ian D. Clark, Ashlie Corcoran, Shannon Currie, Tess Degenstein, Erin Fleck, Virgilia Griffith, Alana Hibbert, Rob Kempson, Cassel Miles, Anand Rajaram, Andrea Scott, Rashida Shaw and Marcel Stewart.

Much thanks to Playwrights Atlantic Resource Centre (PARC) and its Home Delivery Program which paired me with Kim McCaw for a long-distance dramaturgy session. His insight, as a brand new person to the script, was very helpful.

I would also like to thank Leah-Simone Bowen for her gentle, passionate and wise direction, as well as James MacDonald and Western Canada Theatre for the world premiere.

Lastly, I've taught playwriting and led many playwriting workshops over the years. One piece of advice that I give is to write without worrying about staging. I've said, many times: "Create the world you want to see. Leave it up to the director and creative team to make it come to life."

Those words came back to haunt me. As the original Mercy / Patricia, I was cursing Marcia the playwright. It took hours to figure out the transition from Act 1 Scene 7 to Scene 8. The slip-on backless shoes really helped. There were a lot of quick changes, especially for Elizabeth / Robin and Faith / Tia. I am so grateful to Leah, the cast and crew for their patience and determination. It all came to life in ways I could not have imagined. It was exhilarating for all of us.

To all future producers of this play, I wish you the best of luck in your approaches to those quick changes. I wish you the same exhilaration that we felt.

Foreword

On my first reading of the script of Marcia Johnson's *Serving Elizabeth* in the fall of 2019, my mind flashed back to one of my most memorable museum experiences, which was not at the British Museum, the Royal Ontario Museum, nor even the Louvre or the Uffizi, but at the humble People's Story Museum in Edinburgh. There I saw, for example, not merely elegant Victorian ball gowns, but detailed renderings of those who toiled in dreary conditions to create them; not more monuments to a few "great men" but artefacts – in the form of placards and t-shirts – memorializing the many who opposed them. To sum up the appeal of both the People's Story Museum and *Serving Elizabeth*: who doesn't appreciate wrongs righted, especially when the "new" stories are innovatively told?

The impetus to give centre stage to the previously unheard is, in fact, the genesis of this, Johnson's seventh produced stage play. The playwright was moved, after viewing an episode of *The Crown* that is set in Kenya but features no Black characters in speaking roles, to write *Serving Elizabeth* "to give voice to British subjects in Africa who were relegated to the background in the Netflix series," according to the Canadian Play Outlet. Having seen the play in late February of 2020 at the venerable Western Canada Theatre in Kamloops – Tk'emlúps te Secwépemc territory – I can testify that, on both page and stage, Johnson has succeeded in creating an intellectually stimulating, structurally clever, and emotionally engaging play that features characters in their rightful positions, while not sacrificing credibility.

Serving Elizabeth cerebrally engages by juxtaposing fascinating historical events with contemporary issues. The 1952 visit to Kenya by Princess Elizabeth (during which time King George VI died) and the not unrelated impending Mau Mau Uprising are paralleled with contemporary social issues in 2015 London,

England. This is not to suggest the circumstances of the protagon-
ists in the two settings are congruent. However, Mercy's position
as a Black colonial woman, subject to temporary imprisonment
and ongoing financial punishment, who apparently compromises
her ideals by working for the representative of her colonization,
inspires Tia, who, as a young Black Canadian intern in a British
television studio, faces certain barriers of her own.

Much as Johnson reacted to the Netflix series, Tia eventually
defies contemporary colonial attitudes by creating a spirited
alternative to the show on which she is working. Tia reframes
the historical 1952 visit to focus on characters she invents:
Mercy and her daughter, Faith, restaurant proprietors who are
enlisted to cook for the princess. Johnson makes deft use of the
play-within-a-play device. As in earlier plays by other such
eminent Canadian female dramatists as Sharon Pollock (in, for
example, *Blood Relations* in 1981) and Ann-Marie MacDonald
(most notably in *Goodnight Desdemona (Good Morning, Juliet)* in
1988) the device reinforces the work's main theme and reminds
audiences that it is *performance* (not actuality) they are witness-
ing. In *Serving Elizabeth,* the play-within-a-play structure also
functions to underscore the contemporary resonance of the historical depiction. In clever additional layers, Tia is, of course, a
stand-in for the playwright, and, in the original production, the
playwright herself is cast in two roles – neither of which is Tia!
It is a testament to Johnson's artistry that the intricate structure
of *Serving Elizabeth* is executed smoothly.

The play evokes emotional engagement by transcending types
and employing humour. A lesser dramatist might be forgiven
for resorting to stereotypes – Elizabeth and her emissaries, for
example, might invite "bad guy" caricatures and the Kenyans
and Tia downtrodden victim types. Johnson, however, infus-
es her characters with complexity, empathy, and grounding.
Particularly striking are the scenes in which Mercy (with a
pinch of rat poison in the pocket of her apron and both duty
and justice on her mind) confronts the princess, and Tia (who
has done considerable research and some hacking) marches
into her nemesis's fancy home under false pretexts: the out-
comes in each case are unexpected, but credible and delightful.
Both Mercy and Tia stand their ground, and, as they tell their
vital stories, pull off something ultimately more fulfilling than

revenge – satisfaction, with their self-respect intact.

As I write this foreword in April of 2020, during the Covid-19 pandemic – which has brought to the forefront a multitude of social inequities across the world and right here in our own backyards in Canada – my initial admiration for *Serving Elizabeth* has only intensified. Reconnecting with the play has been a welcome reminder of the power of strong, graceful, and well-crafted art to motivate and heal. We, as readers and audiences, owe much to Marcia Johnson for standing *her* ground, Thousand Islands Playhouse and Western Canada Theatre for recognizing a vital story, and Scirocco Drama for having the wisdom to share *Serving Elizabeth* with us.

Ginny Ratsoy is an Associate Professor of English at Thompson Rivers University. She would like to thank Mary Curran for her keen eye and Western Canada Theatre for permission to adapt her program notes for this book.

Production History

Serving Elizabeth premiered at Western Canada Theatre,
February 20–29, 2020.

Cast

Allison Edwards-Crewe .... FAITH / TIA

Marcia Johnson .... MERCY / PATRICIA

Amanda Lisman ..... HRH Princess ELIZABETH / ROBIN

Tony Ofori .... MONTAGUE / STEVEN

Geoffrey Pounsett .... TALBOT / MAURICE

Creative Team

Leah-Simone Bowen – Director

Rachel Forbes – Set and Costume Designer

Jareth Li – Lighting Designer

Andrew Penner – Sound Designer

Christine Leroux – Stage Manager

Cassidy Gallant – Assistant Stage Manager

Characters

	1952:	*2015:*
Actor 1 *Black, female,* *40s–50s*	MERCY *runs a restaurant* *in Nyeri, Kenya*	PATRICIA *casting director* *in London*
Actor 2 *Black, female,* *early 20s*	FAITH *MERCY's* *daughter*	TIA *a Canadian film student* *in London*
Actor 3 *White, male,* *40 plus*	TALBOT, *an envoy to* *Princess* *ELIZABETH*	MAURICE *(pronounced Morris),* *an English writer* MAN *a character from a* *romantic comedy*
Actor 4 *White, female,* *mid 20s*	HRH Princess ELIZABETH	ROBIN *a production manager* *in London* ASHLEY *an actor* WOMAN *a character from a* *romantic comedy*
Actor 5 *Black, male,* *late 20s–mid 30s*	MONTAGUE *driver and assistant* *to TALBOT*	STEVEN *an English actor*

Plus voiceovers of BBC news readers.

Act 1, Scene 1: An Opportunity

> *January 1952. A small restaurant in Nyeri, Kenya. MERCY sits at a table packing away Christmas ornaments. FAITH is on a ladder, halfheartedly taking down garlands.*

FAITH: I do not want to stay at home all day looking after Papa!

MERCY: It will not be all day. Mrs. Otieno has agreed to sit with him in the afternoons.

FAITH: Why not the whole day? Papa likes her.

MERCY: We cannot ask that of a neighbour. Especially at her age.

FAITH: Oh, it is so disgusting.

MERCY: You think there were diamonds in your nappies?

FAITH: I was a baby!

MERCY: Your father did not want to have a stroke, Faith.

FAITH: I know that.

MERCY: You can think of it as practice for when you have babies of your own.

FAITH: That is not funny.

MERCY: It is just until classes start.

FAITH: Eight whole months?!

MERCY: Eight months without a nurse will help to pay for school.

Get down. I will finish.

> *FAITH gets down from the ladder and sulks. MERCY makes quick work of removing the rest of the garlands and putting them away.*

FAITH: Every year, you come up with an excuse for me to defer.

MERCY: Not this year, Faith.

FAITH: That is what you said last year.

MERCY: I want you to get out of here and put that brain of yours to good use just as much as you do.

> *FAITH continues to sulk.*

Finish tidying up.

FAITH: The place is spotless.

MERCY: Did you check the lavatory?

FAITH: Why is it always shit with you?

MERCY: Faith!

FAITH: Yes, I checked the lavatory.

> *A kettle whistles.*

MERCY: Good. Put everything away.

FAITH: All right.

> *MERCY goes to the kitchen. The kettle stops whistling. FAITH takes the Christmas ornaments to a back room. After a moment, TALBOT enters. He carries a briefcase. He studies the place with great curiosity. FAITH re-enters.*

TALBOT: Hello.

FAITH: Hello. Are you lost?

TALBOT: No.

FAITH: What do you want?

TALBOT: I was hoping for a bite to eat.

FAITH: Really?

TALBOT: You are open for business?

FAITH: Yes. Yes.

> MERCY enters.

MERCY: Do you need directions to the main road?

FAITH: He is here for lunch, Mama!

MERCY: We serve only African food.

TALBOT: Yes, I was counting on that.

FAITH: Would you like a glass of water?

TALBOT: A cup of tea would be nice.

FAITH: The water just boiled.

MERCY: I was making tea for myself.

FAITH: I will add more water to the kettle. Excuse me.

> FAITH goes to the kitchen.

TALBOT: May I have a menu, please?

> MERCY points to a blackboard.

Sorry. My Swahili is dreadful.

> FAITH returns with a mug and places it in front of TALBOT.

FAITH: I will translate for you.

MERCY: Fine.

MERCY takes the ladder to the back room.

FAITH: Meat stew with carrots, peas and potatoes with a light tomato base.

TALBOT: What is the meat?

FAITH: Today it is goat.

TALBOT: Interesting.

FAITH: We also have *matoke*: plantain cooked up with tomatoes, onion, chilies, garlic and lemon juice.

TALBOT: Sounds delicious.

FAITH: It is.

TALBOT: Do you also happen to serve *maharagwe*?

FAITH: Oh, yes. But it is quite spicy.

TALBOT: I was told it helps to eat it with *ugali*.

FAITH: You are absolutely right. Shall I bring that for you?

TALBOT: Yes. The meat and plantain dishes as well.

FAITH: Sir, that is a lot of food.

TALBOT: I have enough money.

FAITH: That is not what I meant.

TALBOT: May I wash my hands?

FAITH: Oh, yes. That way.

TALBOT: Thank you. Excuse me.

He goes to the back room, giving a nod to MERCY as she re-enters.

MERCY: Is he making a joke?

FAITH: I do not think so.

MERCY: I should refuse him service.

FAITH: Mama, they are not all like the settlers.

MERCY: It would make a statement.

FAITH: We need the money.

MERCY: No thanks to the English!

FAITH: Please, Mama. Stay in the kitchen. You will not even have to look at him.

MERCY: All right. But I am only doing this to show you that sometimes we have to do things we do not want to do for the greater good.

FAITH: Yes, Mama.

TALBOT re-enters. The kettle whistles.

TALBOT: What a lovely sound.

FAITH: I'll be right back.

MERCY: No. I will go.

MERCY goes to the kitchen.

FAITH: We don't tend to have English people come here.

TALBOT: I got that impression.

FAITH: What brings you to Nyeri?

TALBOT: Business.

FAITH: Are you with the mineral water company? We
              keep hearing that they will be building a factory
              here.

TALBOT: No. Nothing like that.

FAITH: Oh. That's too bad.

TALBOT: You want a noisy building site so close to you?

FAITH: The builders need to eat.

TALBOT: Oh, yes.

FAITH: And when the workers start, we will feed them
              too.

TALBOT: Has business been slow for you?

              MERCY enters with the teapot.

MERCY: Business is just fine. You do not need to concern
              yourself with our affairs.

TALBOT: I am pleased to hear that you are doing well.

MERCY: Are you?

TALBOT: Why, yes.

MERCY: Hm.

              MERCY goes back to the kitchen.

FAITH: Don't mind Mama.

TALBOT: She seems like a sensible, hard-working woman.

FAITH: But not always very friendly.

TALBOT: You make a good team.

FAITH: Thank you.

              TALBOT checks inside the teapot.

TALBOT: Another minute or two.

MERCY: (*From the kitchen.*) Stew!

FAITH: I'll be right back.

> *She leaves for the kitchen. TALBOT takes a notebook and pen from inside his jacket. FAITH returns with a bowl, which she places in front of him.*

Here you are.

TALBOT: It smells divine.

FAITH: Enjoy.

> *He eats a spoonful.*

TALBOT: The flavour lives up to the aroma.

FAITH: Mama will be so pleased that you like it.

TALBOT: What's next?

FAITH: Everything's hot so I can bring whatever you like when you're ready.

TALBOT: You can bring it all at once.

FAITH: You don't want to finish the stew?

TALBOT: No, that was quite enough.

FAITH: Oh. If you're sure.

TALBOT: Yes, thank you.

> *She takes the bowl.*

FAITH: All right.

> *A bewildered FAITH exits to the kitchen with the bowl. TALBOT makes notes. MERCY storms out of the kitchen, spoon in hand,*

> *ready to confront him. FAITH runs in and grabs her, pulling her back into the kitchen. TALBOT is oblivious. After a moment, FAITH enters, carrying a tray with several dishes on it and places them in front of him.*

TALBOT: Well done.

FAITH: Here is the *matoke* and this is the *maharagwe* with the *ugali*.

TALBOT: Splendid!

FAITH: Well, enjoy.

> *FAITH goes to the kitchen. TALBOT eats and makes notes. After a moment, both FAITH and MERCY peer out at him, studying him. He senses that he's being watched and turns around but misses MERCY as she ducks back into the kitchen. FAITH begins to wipe down her serving tray with a great deal of focus. She gives him a nod and he nods back. He takes a few more bites before writing in his notebook. He takes a folder from his briefcase and places it on the table. FAITH goes to him.*

Do you like everything?

TALBOT: Delicious. The best food that I've had in Kenya.

FAITH: Oh, good.

TALBOT: You may take it away.

FAITH: All right, if you're sure.

TALBOT: Yes, thank you. I would like to see your mother if she has a moment.

FAITH: I will ask her.

FAITH exits with the dishes. Talbot pours a cup of tea and drinks from it. MERCY enters. She is perturbed. FAITH follows, worried.

MERCY: Now, see here!

TALBOT: Ah, Mrs. Nyanjiru.

MERCY: How did you know my name?

TALBOT: Your reputation precedes you.

MERCY: Who are you?

TALBOT: Lester Talbot. Will you have a seat? You as well, Faith.

FAITH: What's going on?

He puts money on the table.

TALBOT: For my bill. With a gratuity for your time.

FAITH: Thank you!

FAITH grabs the money, puts it in her apron pocket and sits. She tugs at her mother's hand encouraging her to sit, which she does.

TALBOT: I have a business opportunity for you, Mrs. Nyanjiru.

MERCY: This is how it always starts.

FAITH: Mama! Please, Mr. Talbot. What is the opportunity?

TALBOT: Have you heard of The Royal Lodge?

MERCY: Its proper name is Sagana Lodge.

TALBOT: Yes, that's the one. I represent people who will be staying there next month. They will need someone to cook authentic Kenyan food for them.

MERCY: There is already a chef there.

TALBOT: He did not meet our security criteria.

MERCY: A criminal?

TALBOT: No, not really.

FAITH: Who are the guests?

TALBOT: I can only share their identities once your mother signs this agreement.

MERCY: I'm just a cook.

TALBOT: You are a very fine cook.

MERCY: You hardly ate anything.

TALBOT: I had lunch before getting here.

MERCY: Why would you waste food and money that way?

TALBOT: I did not want hunger to sway my judgment.

FAITH: That makes sense. Doesn't it, Mama?

TALBOT: I will have a chance to truly savour your meals at the Lodge. We are taking over the entire facility for a week. One month from tomorrow.

MERCY: I cannot leave this business unattended for that long.

TALBOT: You will be compensated for the revenue you would have earned here.

            TALBOT slides the agreement to her.

MERCY: That is the payment and compensation combined?

TALBOT: No, that is the fee for your cooking services alone. We would pay you this additional amount here for closing your restaurant temporarily.

FAITH: *Kamae!*

MERCY: Faith!

FAITH: Sorry.

TALBOT: You will get there a week ahead of them so you can learn to cook a few of their favourite dishes before they arrive from England.

MERCY: You said they wanted Kenyan food.

TALBOT: They might want a familiar meal from home on occasion. Recipes will be provided. I have been assured that they are very easy to follow.

MERCY: I never use recipes.

TALBOT: But, you can read?

MERCY: Of course I can read.

TALBOT: Forgive me. Is there anything else I may answer for you?

MERCY: It would not take me a week to learn how to cook English meals.

TALBOT: We would require you to undergo other training as well.

MERCY: Training for what?

TALBOT: I'm afraid that I can only disclose that when you have signed.

FAITH: You have to know tonight?

TALBOT: It would make my life much easier.

MERCY: Why must we always make life easier for Englishmen?

FAITH: Mama!

TALBOT: It is true that our presence has not always served the natives well.

MERCY: No, it has not!

TALBOT: Are you saying no outright?

FAITH: No, she isn't. Can you give us a few minutes to talk?

TALBOT: Yes, of course. I should have thought of that.

FAITH: Thank you so much, Mr. Talbot. Let me top up your tea.

TALBOT: Oh, yes, please. What is this brew, by the way?

MERCY: Just tea.

FAITH: From our family tea garden.

TALBOT: Delightful.

                    He exits the restaurant.

FAITH: It's some rich tourist, I bet. A movie star! Like Greer Garson or Laurence Olivier!

MERCY: I never thought that a daughter of mine would be so fascinated by the English.

FAITH: Times have changed, Mama.

MERCY: Many people would consider me a traitor if I did this.

FAITH: Well, they are not going to pay my tuition or boarding fees, are they?

MERCY: I wonder how big the kitchen at Sagana Lodge is.

FAITH: Probably the size of this restaurant.

MERCY: Hm.

FAITH: We could afford a nurse again.

MERCY: A few days a week, maybe.

FAITH: Then it's decided.

MERCY: Let me think for a minute.

FAITH: (*Overlapping, yelling.*) Mr. Talbot!

MERCY: Faith.

FAITH: What?

                      TALBOT enters.

TALBOT: Well?

FAITH: Mama?

MERCY: All right. I will cook for your clients.

TALBOT: Excellent. Here you are. (*MERCY signs the papers.*) I will need your signature too, Miss. Nyanjiru.

FAITH: Yes, I'm happy to.

TALBOT: Just here, under your mother's.

                      FAITH signs. TALBOT checks the form and puts it in his folder.

              You might want to sit down.

MERCY: Please just tell me.

TALBOT: Right then. The guests at the Royal Lodge –
             excuse me, the Sagana Lodge – will be Their
             Royal Highnesses Princess Elizabeth and Philip,
             Duke of Edinburgh.

MERCY: No.

FAITH: *Kamae!*

MERCY: Faith!

FAITH: Sorry.

TALBOT: Which is why you will need the additional
             training. Comportment lessons.

MERCY: I would be learning to curtsy?

TALBOT: Among other things, yes.

MERCY: May I look at the agreement again?

TALBOT: Yes, of course.

             *TALBOT hands her the document. She rips
             it up.*

FAITH: Mama, no!

TALBOT: Mrs. Nyanjiru.

MERCY: I will not serve that woman.

TALBOT: Please, let's talk about this. Mrs. Nyanjiru!

             MERCY has gone to the kitchen.

FAITH: I knew that it was too good to be true.

TALBOT: Why would she not want to serve the princess?

FAITH: We are from Murang'a.

TALBOT: I don't believe I know it.

FAITH: Fort Hall?

Mercy (Marcia Johnson) and Faith (Allison Edwards-Crewe) talk about caring for their husband / father.

Mercy (Marcia Johnson) shocks Faith (Allison Edwards-Crewe) and Talbot (Geoffrey Pounsett).

TALBOT: Oh!

FAITH: Yes.

TALBOT: She was part of the women's revolt?

FAITH: Yes.

TALBOT: Terrible business.

FAITH: Mama blames the King for not doing anything about it.

TALBOT: And the Princess by extension.

FAITH: I'm sorry.

TALBOT: Do you think that you can get her to change her mind?

FAITH: You still want to hire her?

TALBOT: More than ever. Her Royal Highness represents the Commonwealth of the future; replacing the imperial past.

FAITH: Oh.

TALBOT: I would hate to start looking again.

FAITH: I will do my best.

TALBOT: Here is another copy of the agreement. I return to London at the end of next week but she can mail it to our office in Nairobi. The address is on the envelope.

FAITH: It might take me a long time to convince her.

TALBOT: Do you have access to a telephone?

FAITH: There's one across the street.

He gives her a business card.

TALBOT: Good. If you need to, just call this number and we'll send someone to collect it. Good luck to you.

FAITH: Thanks.

TALBOT begins to pick up the ripped-up paper from the floor.

Oh, don't bother. I will do that.

TALBOT: I'm afraid that I have to do it myself. But, there is something that you could do.

FAITH: Yes?

TALBOT: Tea is still under rationing at home.

He takes out some money.

FAITH: Oh, that's too much.

TALBOT: Consider it a bonus.

FAITH: Thank you, sir. (*Giving him a packet.*) Here you are.

TALBOT: Wonderful!

Goodbye. It was lovely to meet you.

FAITH: Thank you. Goodbye, sir.

TALBOT exits.

He's gone!

MERCY enters with two mugs.

MERCY: Good riddance.

She sits and begins drinking her tea.

Your tea is getting cold.

FAITH joins her.

FAITH: I heard that royals stay in grand hotels.

MERCY: Did you, now?

FAITH: They even travel with personal chefs.

MERCY: Hm.

FAITH: But Princess Elizabeth wants to hire you. That shows respect.

MERCY: It is not enough.

FAITH: It's a start. She's representing the Commonwealth of the future and not the... um... the colonial, the imperialism...

MERCY: The imperial past.

FAITH: You were listening!

MERCY: I stopped after he said that. What nonsense.

FAITH: Did you hear that he doesn't care about Murang'a? He still wants to engage you.

MERCY: Only because he's too lazy to look for someone else.

FAITH: Who are we to turn our backs on this gift? God works in mysterious ways.

MERCY: And now God has made his way into the discussion.

FAITH: Well... He does.

MERCY: Does this mean that I will see you at church next week?

FAITH: Maybe you will.

MERCY: A true miracle!

FAITH: They want to make amends. Look how much he gave me for a little bit of tea.

MERCY: It's a pittance! Some of the jewels in the King's crown come from our land. We don't get to keep anything for ourselves!

FAITH: So your answer is definitely no.

MERCY: It is. Let's not talk about it anymore.

FAITH: All right, Mama.

MERCY: He left his folder.

FAITH: Yes. I'm keeping it for school. One less thing to buy.

MERCY: You're finally learning.

FAITH: Yes, Mama.

They continue to drink their tea in silence.

Act 1, Scene 2: A Fan of Princesses

> *Production office. London, England, 2015.*
> *TIA is sorting through and collating script*
> *pages while occasionally flipping through*
> *a magazine. ROBIN enters with two travel*
> *mugs.*

ROBIN: Break time!

TIA: Oh, you didn't have to.

ROBIN: I'd get coffee over sorting through that mess any day.

TIA: It's not so bad.

ROBIN: Will you not stop?

TIA: I don't want to lose my place.

ROBIN: You're worth every penny we're paying you.

TIA: Very funny.

ROBIN: And you do it all while reading *Hello!*

TIA: Kate's baby bump is finally showing.

ROBIN: Is it?

TIA: This pregnancy is going more smoothly than her first one.

ROBIN: I'm sure that she's doing just fine.

TIA: Done!

> *She joins ROBIN on the couch and picks up*
> *the travel mug.*

ROBIN: Two creams, two sugars?

TIA: Perfect. (*Re: mug.*) Ooh, the company logo. Can I keep this?

ROBIN: Of course.

TIA: Thanks, Robin.

ROBIN: It's the least I could do. If the scripts had gone out that way... Nightmare. We're well rid of what's his name.

TIA: Gabe. He's not a bad guy.

ROBIN: One script had two page threes and no page four. It's like he was trying to be let go.

TIA: I don't think that this project was manly enough for him.

ROBIN: Well, I hope that he and Double-O-Seven are very happy together.

TIA: Last I heard, he was locking down walking tours on London Bridge during filming.

ROBIN: Nightmare. Serves him right.

TIA: Why don't you send the files to a print shop? Wouldn't even have to leave the office.

ROBIN: And some entrepreneur would leak the whole thing.

TIA: Oh, yeah.

ROBIN: Let's just enjoy this moment of quiet before everyone comes back.

TIA: Why didn't you go?

ROBIN: Every friend or relative who visits me insists on going to Buckingham Bloody Palace. I've reached my saturation point.

TIA: We're not actually filming there, are we?

ROBIN: Lancaster House is standing in. They just wanted to get a feel for the real palace. Team-building exercise, I think. Sorry that I couldn't spare you.

TIA: Already been there. Got a keychain.

ROBIN: Of course you did.

> *TIA holds up the magazine showing a picture of Prince George.*

TIA: He is so adorable.

ROBIN: Hm.

TIA: I saw Kate and William when they visited Canada.

ROBIN: So you said.

TIA: It was their first trip after the wedding.

ROBIN: Did your mother line up to see Prince Edward in Toronto?

TIA: Yes! Oh, I've already told you.

ROBIN: A few times. Have you always been a fan?

TIA: I was a princess every year for Hallowe'en.

ROBIN: Aren't you supposed to dress up as ghouls or vampires?

TIA: Not in my world.

ROBIN: I wouldn't switch places with Kate Middleton for all the tea in China.

TIA: I don't know. I like the idea of never having to make my bed.

ROBIN: So, don't make your bed.

TIA: I mean, like being on a cruise. You leave your room for five minutes and someone comes in and tidies everything up. You never have to cook for yourself. They know how you take your coffee...

ROBIN: This show is the perfect placement for you.

TIA: I know!

ROBIN: By the way... The finance department okayed the trip to Africa.

TIA: But Elizabeth practically turned right back around as soon as she got there.

ROBIN: Well, enough happened for an hour of telly. Or streaming. Whatever we're supposed to call it. And you get to come with us!

TIA: What about school?

ROBIN: I've cleared it. You'll get all kinds of extra credit.

TIA: Cool.

ROBIN: That's it?

TIA: What?

ROBIN: I just got you an all expenses paid trip to the other side of the world!

TIA: Right. Sorry. Thanks so much.

ROBIN: Do you have something against Africa?

TIA: No! I was born in Kenya.

ROBIN: What?

TIA: Yeah. I speak Kiswahili and a little Kikuyu.

ROBIN: *Key* Swahili?

TIA: That's the language that Swahili people speak.

ROBIN: You're full of surprises. And no accent at all. No African accent, I mean.

TIA: I was a baby when we moved to Toronto. I've gone back almost every summer.

ROBIN: So, going there is like going to Buckingham Bloody Palace.

TIA: Well, Nyeri's a bit bigger.

ROBIN: Did you say Nyeri? Where Elizabeth was staying when she found out that she was queen?

TIA: Didn't you read my essay?

ROBIN: I'll get right on that.

TIA: Robin!

ROBIN: I knew you'd be better than What's-His-Name.

TIA: Gabe.

ROBIN: Doesn't matter.

TIA: Are we going to the actual locations?

ROBIN: We're not even going to Kenya. South Africa gave us a better deal.

                    PATRICIA runs in flustered.

TIA: Hi, Patricia.

ROBIN: Hey, what are you doing here?

PATRICIA: Bad news.

ROBIN: What is it? You look dreadful.

TIA: I'll get you a glass of water.

PATRICIA/ROBIN: Thanks.

TIA exits.

ROBIN: Well?

PATRICIA: We've lost Elizabeth.

ROBIN: What do you mean, lost her?

PATRICIA: I mean it's back to the bloody drawing board.

ROBIN: All right. Slow down and tell me what happened.

Act 1, Scene 3: An Invitation for a Drive

> *January, 1952. Restaurant in Nyeri. FAITH is wiping down the chalkboard. She doesn't notice when MONTAGUE enters. He sees her but takes a moment to check his reflection in a window and straighten his tie.*

MONTAGUE: Good day.

FAITH: Oh, good day. I will clean a table for you.

MONTAGUE: There is no need.

FAITH: You cannot sit at a dirty table.

> *FAITH quickly cleans a table.*

MONTAGUE: Thank you.

> *He sits.*

FAITH: Would you like a glass of water?

MONTAGUE: That would be very nice. The road was quite dusty.

FAITH: Right away, Mr...?

MONTAGUE: Mwangi. But please call me by my first name.

FAITH: All right.

> *Before he can tell her his name, FAITH goes to the kitchen and comes back very quickly with a glass of water.*

Here you are.

MONTAGUE: Montague.

FAITH: What?

MONTAGUE: That is my first name. It's French.

FAITH: Oh. My name is Faith.

MONTAGUE: Pleasure.

MONTAGUE drinks.

FAITH: We're officially closed until supper but I can serve you some *pilau* or *ugali.*

MONTAGUE: Oh, I am not here to eat. Is your mother present?

FAITH: She went to the market.

MONTAGUE: Do you know how long she will be?

FAITH: Half an hour maybe. It depends on how many friends she stops to chat with.

MONTAGUE: Oh, yes. My mother is the same way.

FAITH: May I help you with something?

MONTAGUE: I have a delivery for her.

FAITH: I always sign for deliveries when she isn't here.

MONTAGUE: Not this time, if you wouldn't mind.

FAITH: Oh. All right.

She begins to clean the other tables.

MONTAGUE: I hope that you have not taken offence.

FAITH: No, I understand.

MONTAGUE: Oh, good.

FAITH: I might break it. Or set it on fire.

MONTAGUE: You are offended, indeed. Maybe I should wait in the car.

FAITH: You have a car?

MONTAGUE: Not mine exactly. It comes with my position.

FAITH runs to the door.

FAITH: Oh, it is so shiny.

MONTAGUE: It is a Rolls-Royce.

FAITH: Do you drive it every day?

MONTAGUE: Very nearly.

FAITH: It must go as fast as the wind.

MONTAGUE: It has a powerful engine.

FAITH: I have only ridden in a car one time.

MONTAGUE: Not even a taxicab?

FAITH: Well, yes, lots of those. But, I was in a regular car only once.

MONTAGUE: What was the occasion?

FAITH: It was when my father had a stroke.

MONTAGUE: I'm sorry.

FAITH: Thank you.

MONTAGUE: Is your father… I don't mean to pry.

FAITH: He is paralyzed on one side.

MONTAGUE: But he is still of sound mind?

FAITH: His memory is not always good, but it's still him. It would have been worse if we hadn't gotten to the hospital so quickly.

MONTAGUE: Whose car was it?

FAITH: A rich white man. He saw Papa collapse as he was driving by.

MONTAGUE: You don't hear stories like that too often.

FAITH: What is your position?

MONTAGUE: I am a driver and assistant for the government.

FAITH: What's that like?

MONTAGUE: It will do for now.

FAITH: What do you want to do?

MONTAGUE: Something that fits in closer with my degree.

FAITH: You went to university?

MONTAGUE: Yes.

FAITH: I'm going too. In the fall. To Egerton.

MONTAGUE: Oh, yes. It has a very good agricultural program.

FAITH: Did you go there?

MONTAGUE: No. I went to Cambridge.

FAITH: Oh.

MONTAGUE: You are eighteen?

FAITH: I'm twenty-one!

MONTAGUE: I have offended you again.

FAITH: I have been helping my mother since Papa's stroke.

MONTAGUE: You are a good daughter.

FAITH: Yes, I am very trustworthy.

MONTAGUE: I am sure that you are.

FAITH: You must have better things to do than watch me clean.

MONTAGUE: There are worse ways to spend an afternoon.

FAITH: Can you at least tell me what's in the package?

MONTAGUE: Documents.

FAITH: From Mr. Talbot?

MONTAGUE: Yes, actually.

FAITH: I was at the meeting with Mr. Talbot and my
              mother. He trusted me to talk my mother into
              changing her mind.

MONTAGUE: The documents arrived in Nairobi yesterday.

FAITH: It worked.

MONTAGUE: What worked?

FAITH: The post. It got to you in time.

MONTAGUE: Yes.

FAITH: Good.

MONTAGUE: I drove him that day; when he made the offer.

FAITH: I didn't see you.

MONTAGUE: I saw you.

FAITH: You did?

MONTAGUE: You were very good at carrying all those dishes.

FAITH: Oh. Thank you.

MONTAGUE: Will you let me take you for a drive?

FAITH: Why?

MONTAGUE: You have only been in a car to go to a hospital.
              That is not right.

FAITH: I am supposed to have everything spotless for
              the supper hour.

MONTAGUE: Looks clean to me.

FAITH: You don't have my mother's eye.

MONTAGUE: I'll have you back in twenty minutes.

FAITH: …

MONTAGUE: When we get back, I will give you the documents.

FAITH: I accept!

> *She takes off her apron. He holds out his arm to her. She takes it and they start their exit.*

MONTAGUE: Where do you want to go?

FAITH: Anywhere!

> *They leave the restaurant.*

Act 1, Scene 4: A Script Is Delivered

> *2015. Production office. MAURICE is meeting with ROBIN.*

MAURICE: You're sure Gambon isn't available?

ROBIN: I'm sure.

MAURICE: Can't picture the other fellow.

ROBIN: You don't like that he's American.

MAURICE: It's preposterous.

ROBIN: He'll be fabulous.

MAURICE: What does the writer's opinion count for, anyway?

ROBIN: Your opinion matters a great deal to us, Mr. Gilder.

MAURICE: Need my blessing, do you?

ROBIN: It would be nice.

MAURICE: What if I don't give it?

ROBIN: We would be very disappointed.

MAURICE: But it wouldn't change anything.

ROBIN: The director and producer have final say, I'm afraid.

MAURICE: Thought so.

ROBIN: Trust me. He'll be great.

MAURICE: Will there be an accent coach on set?

ROBIN: Absolutely.

MAURICE: All right. Go on, then.

ROBIN: Oh, thank you so much, Mr. Gilder.

MAURICE: I'm a bit on edge after the Elizabeth incident.

ROBIN: Very unfortunate.

MAURICE: I trust that we sent flowers?

ROBIN: A gift basket.

MAURICE: Can't we delay production at all?

ROBIN: It's a compound fracture, I'm afraid. She'll be in physiotherapy for months after the cast comes off.

MAURICE: Damn shame.

ROBIN: She's lucky she didn't break her neck.

MAURICE: What on earth was she thinking, going riding so close to filming?

ROBIN: She wanted to brush up on her skills. Can't really blame her.

MAURICE: Her audition tape was absolutely brilliant.

ROBIN: It was, but, Mr. Gilder, there is no shortage of young actresses who would fit the bill.

MAURICE: I hope that you're right.

ROBIN: We've narrowed it down to two.

MAURICE: Is that so?

ROBIN: I'm leaning toward this one. Her name's Ashley. Just three years out of college.

             ROBIN shows him a photo and résumé. He looks at the photo.

MAURICE: Perfect colouring.

ROBIN: Her credits are impressive.

               He turns over the photo to look at the résumé.
               It's not clear that he can read it.

MAURICE: Well, yes. Excellent for one so young.

               He hands it back to ROBIN.

ROBIN: We're in really good shape, Mr. Gilder.

MAURICE: Well, I shall take your word for it.

ROBIN: I appreciate that.

MAURICE: Lovely to see you again, my dear. Let me know
               if you'd like tickets to the play.

ROBIN: Oh, how generous.

MAURICE: Not at all. There tend to be good seats on
               weeknights.

ROBIN: I'll check with Pat.

MAURICE: Oh, yes. Well, I hope that you both enjoy it.

ROBIN: Aren't you forgetting something?

MAURICE: Eh?

ROBIN: The Kenya script.

MAURICE: Oh, I didn't give it to you?

ROBIN: No.

MAURICE: Where's my head?

               He sits again and makes quite a production
               of finding his reading glasses, bringing
               the briefcase onto his lap, working the
               combination lock, etc.

ROBIN: I really appreciate you bringing it all the way here but you could have sent a PDF.

MAURICE: Couldn't risk being hacked again.

ROBIN: We could have sent a courier.

MAURICE: After all the back and forth on this one, I wanted to make sure that it went directly from my hands to yours.

ROBIN: Well, thank you. (*Re: lock.*) Do you need help with that?

MAURICE: The lighting is so blessedly dim in these offices.

ROBIN: Say no more.

                She activates her cell phone flashlight and shines it on the lock.

MAURICE: Just the thing.

                He unlocks the case and takes out the script. ROBIN reaches for it. He doesn't seem to be able to part with it yet.

                There was a part of me that felt that I would never finish this one.

ROBIN: I'm sure that it's wonderful.

MAURICE: In any case, I apologize for being so late with it.

                He finally gives the script to her.

ROBIN: Thank you so much. And no apology necessary. It's remarkable to have only one writer for all ten episodes. You've done amazing work.

MAURICE: Well, yes. That's good to hear.

                He lingers.

ROBIN: I trust that you'll be coming to Africa with us.

MAURICE: Wouldn't miss it.

> *ROBIN gets a flyer from her desk and hands it to MAURICE.*

ROBIN: Here's the travel clinic we're using.

MAURICE: I have to get shots?

ROBIN: Everyone does. Except my assistant, Tia.

MAURICE: Why ever not?

ROBIN: She's originally from Africa. Was there only last summer.

MAURICE: Oh, good thinking.

ROBIN: It was completely by accident.

MAURICE: Providence then.

ROBIN: Yes. We're lucky to have her.

MAURICE: Where is she?

ROBIN: Tesco. We're out of loo rolls.

MAURICE: Oh, the glamour of filmmaking.

ROBIN: Don't know what I'd do without her.

MAURICE: Where's everyone else?

ROBIN: We're moving office to Lancaster House.

MAURICE: Working out of trailers, then.

ROBIN: Hence the loo rolls. It'll be nice to get out of London, anyway.

MAURICE: Yes, I'd better get to Waterloo before the unwashed masses descend.

ROBIN: Thanks again. I really look forward to reading it.

MAURICE: Yes. Yes.

ROBIN: I'll walk you out.

As they exit.

MAURICE: Oh, thank you. This place is a bit of a rabbit warren.

ROBIN: Oh, I know.

As ROBIN turns to place the script on her desk, she drops her fan girl persona for a moment. She revs it back up as she follows MAURICE.

(*From off.*) I got lost a dozen times my first week here.

Suddenly the lights go out.

MAURICE: (*From off.*) Oh, bloody hell!

Act 1, Scene 5: The Princess Is Briefed

> *January, 1952. Clarence House in London. TALBOT seems impatient. He looks through his notes, checks his watch and looks down the hallway. Finally he sits in one of the opulent chairs. ELIZABETH arrives, putting on a cardigan. TALBOT immediately stands and bows to her.*

ELIZABETH: So sorry to keep you waiting, Talbot.

TALBOT: Not at all.

ELIZABETH: Where were we?

TALBOT: The governor.

ELIZABETH: Oh, yes. Sir Philip Euen Mitchell.

TALBOT: Well done.

ELIZABETH: His Christian name is easy enough to remember, Philip. His wife wouldn't be called Elizabeth, would she?

TALBOT: Quite amusing, ma'am. But, no. Her name is Mary Catherine.

ELIZABETH: Named after two queens.

TALBOT: Likes to be called Katie.

ELIZABETH: Katie.

TALBOT: How long has Philip Euen Mitchell been governor of the Kenya colony?

ELIZABETH: Since nineteen forty-five?

TALBOT: Forty-four.

ELIZABETH: Forty-four! Yes, I knew that.

TALBOT: Well done, ma'am. He will greet you on the airfield along with the RAF Guard of Honour and approximately four hundred tribal chiefs.

ELIZABETH: My word.

TALBOT: Apparently it will take days for some of those chiefs to walk there.

ELIZABETH: Well, I hope that they will all think that I was worth it.

TALBOT: Of course they will. After the greeting, you will be directed to a dais to make your first speech.

He hands a speech to her.

ELIZABETH: You already gave it to me.

TALBOT: An addition has been made.

ELIZABETH: Oh, I see it. "Nairobi was a savage place, the home of wild animals and uninhabited except for the occasional band of nomadic herdsman. Now it is a modern vibrant city."

TALBOT: Yes, that's it.

ELIZABETH: Hm.

TALBOT: Problem?

ELIZABETH: No, it's very good I can't help but wonder about the timing of this trip, though.

TALBOT: Ma'am.

ELIZABETH: Kenya is so very far away.

TALBOT: May I remind you that you and the Duke are going in order to avoid cancelling a royal visit altogether.

ELIZABETH: Surely we can postpone. Only for a month or
               two?

TALBOT: The Kenyan people were so looking forward
               to seeing the King. But I daresay they are even
               more excited that you and the Duke are going
               instead.

ELIZABETH: You're just saying that.

TALBOT: They gave you an extraordinary number of
               wedding gifts. To cancel on them now…

ELIZABETH: How many gifts?

TALBOT: In excess of twenty-five hundred.

ELIZABETH: My word.

TALBOT: Including the Royal Lodge in Nyeri.

               He shows her a photo.

ELIZABETH: Looks lovely. Did you visit it?

TALBOT: I did, ma'am, and it is indeed lovely.

ELIZABETH: Maybe we can put off Australia and New
               Zealand?

TALBOT: Ma'am.

ELIZABETH: Or Ceylon?

TALBOT: Ceylon hasn't had a royal visit in over fifty years.

ELIZABETH: Oh.

               I am not only thinking of myself.

TALBOT: Yes, I'm sure that you will miss your children.

ELIZABETH: They will be in good hands. But the Duke was
               so looking forward to going back to Malta.

TALBOT: Yes, that part is disappointing.

ELIZABETH: I do wish that we could all go together. Papa included.

TALBOT: I am afraid that it would be quite impossible for His Majesty to be on an airplane in his condition. The Queen, of course, will stay behind with him.

ELIZABETH: Yes, naturally. Well, thank goodness for my husband. I was never more grateful for him than on our last trip. I was out of my depth.

TALBOT: What do you mean? You were a sensation in Canada and the US!

ELIZABETH: Not according to *Time* magazine.

TALBOT: You were not meant to see that.

ELIZABETH: Well, I did. "Elizabeth is unlikely to match the tremendous personal success scored by her mother on her 1939 visit."

TALBOT: An unfair comparison.

ELIZABETH: They said I was stiff! And I missed Charles's birthday. Again.

TALBOT: You seemed quite the natural by the end. Perfect training for this trip. Shall we continue?

ELIZABETH: If we must

TALBOT: After your speech, you and the Duke will ride in an open car throughout the streets of Nairobi.

ELIZABETH: Where we shall wave and smile.

TALBOT: To the delight of thousands of people lining the route. Then on to the children's hospital.

ELIZABETH: I'm so glad that it has been completed.

TALBOT: You will meet a few of the healthier, mobile patients.

ELIZABETH: Poor dears. Please remind me to pick up gifts for Charles and Anne.

TALBOT: Something made by real African artisans?

ELIZABETH: Oh, yes. Charles loves lions.

TALBOT: And Princess Anne?

ELIZABETH: Horses, of course.

TALBOT: A toy zebra, perhaps?

ELIZABETH: What would I do without you, Talbot?

TALBOT: It's my pleasure, Your Highness. After the hospital, you will go on safari and stay at The Treetops. Your quarters will be high above the savannah with an ideal view of an elephant watering hole.

ELIZABETH: This trip is growing on me, Talbot.

TALBOT: Glad to hear it.

ELIZABETH: Sir Mitchell has had this post since forty-four and his lovely wife goes by the name of Katie.

TALBOT: Splendid.

A clock chimes.

ELIZABETH: Excellent. Time for tea.

TALBOT: I must endeavour to not get caught up in conversation during our briefings.

ELIZABETH: Oh dear. That does make me sound naughty.

TALBOT: No, Your Highness. I would never say such a thing.

ELIZABETH: Calm down, Talbot. I was only teasing. Shall we continue in half an hour?

TALBOT: I was hoping that we could continue with the briefing while having our tea. Time is of the essence.

ELIZABETH: (*Sighs.*) Yes, well. All right then.

                She rises and begins to leave.

TALBOT: Ma'am?

ELIZABETH: Tea is served down the hall.

TALBOT: Right. Yes, ma'am.

                He looks at the ridiculous amount of paperwork that is laid out on the table.

ELIZABETH: See you shortly.

                He bows. She exits. He starts picking up his carefully laid out lesson plan. The impatience from the beginning of the scene has returned.

Act 1, Scene 6: Tia the Writer

> *2015. Production office. The power is still out. TIA is shining a flashlight on a script as she and ROBIN read from it.*

TIA: "Can this really be happening?"

ROBIN: "Believe me. I never thought that I would settle down with anyone."

TIA: "What makes me so special?"

ROBIN: "Don't you know?"

TIA: "I'm just an ordinary girl from Kansas."

ROBIN: "You may be from Kansas, but..."

> *This prospect of continuing is really painful for ROBIN.*

TIA: Keep going.

ROBIN: "You may be from Kansas, but there is absolutely nothing ordinary about you."

TIA: "He takes her in his arms and they gaze into each other's eyes before he envelops her in a passionate embrace. The music swells. They come out of the kiss and..."

ROBIN: "I'm ready to settle down if you are."

TIA: "You'd better believe it, Captain. He picks her up in his arms. The camera pans out and, in a drone shot, we see the sailboat lolling on the ocean while Christian carries Alex below deck. The end."

ROBIN: Well.

TIA: Come on, Robin. It's the perfect rom-com.

ROBIN: Typical, more like.

TIA: Even better.

ROBIN: You're aiming for typical?

TIA: Yeah! I want to appeal to those doe-eyed girls who pick the movie on a first date.

ROBIN: At least you know your demographic.

TIA: Everyone else aims for eighteen- to forty-nine-year-old males...

ROBIN: Eighteen- to forty-nine-year-old white males.

TIA: Whatever.

ROBIN: And it's worth noting that studios won't give lead roles to Black actors unless you state it in the script. And usually not even then.

TIA: They can cast who they want.

ROBIN: You really mean that?

TIA: Whatever it takes to get it made.

ROBIN: If you don't mind me saying...

TIA: What?

ROBIN: This reminds me of your obsession with the royal family.

TIA: I wouldn't say that I'm obsessed.

ROBIN: Well, I find it odd for someone from Kenya to be a fan of the monarchy.

TIA: It runs in the family. My grandparents have a commemorative portrait in their front hall.

ROBIN: Seriously?

TIA: The royal couple put Nyeri on the map.

ROBIN: And you say that without irony.

TIA: What do you have against the royals?

ROBIN: For one thing, I don't think that anyone's born better than anyone else.

TIA: Well, yeah…

ROBIN: And England has a lot to answer for when it comes to countries like Kenya.

TIA: But Kenya did get its independence!

ROBIN: After fighting bloody rebellions to get out from under British rule.

TIA: And then came one corrupt government after another.

ROBIN: Are you saying that you preferred Kenya being a colony?

TIA: Well, neither system's perfect.

ROBIN: That's the understatement of the century.

TIA: Why are you mad at me?

ROBIN: I'm not mad – Look, the monarchy is not a fairy tale. It's a relic that should have been dismantled centuries ago.

TIA: But it's part of your heritage.

ROBIN: So was The Plague.

TIA: England has changed.

ROBIN: Too much for some. Brexit's going to take us back to the "good old days."

TIA: There's no way that people will vote to leave the EU.

ROBIN: If you say so. When are the bloody lights coming back on?

TIA checks her computer.

TIA: Server's still down too.

A moment.

ROBIN: We're okay, right?

TIA: Yeah.

ROBIN: Really?

TIA: I like that you don't talk to me like I'm a lowly intern.

ROBIN: If you couldn't tell, I'm not a fan of classism.

TIA: I will rise up from my humble origins.

ROBIN: 'Course you will.

TIA: Starting with *Sailing into Love*?

ROBIN: Well…

TIA: Is it commercial? Will it get my name out there and pay me enough money to make my own indie?

ROBIN: I'll just get my Tarot cards, shall I?

TIA: Robin, your opinion means a lot to me. I can take it.

ROBIN: Well, you asked for it. Too many locations, logistical nightmare filming on the water, audiences will get confused with all the subplots and it's way too short.

TIA: I could make it longer.

ROBIN: God, no.

TIA: That bad?

ROBIN: You said you could take it.

TIA: Yeah, I did.

ROBIN: What's the film you really want to make?

TIA: Well, you won't believe me, but my whole life I've wanted to write about the royal visit to Nyeri.

ROBIN: Have you started working on it?

TIA: About three years ago. I wrote a scene as part of my application for school.

ROBIN: As opposed to the two weeks it took you to write the rom-com?

TIA: How did you know?

ROBIN: I can tell when a writer's thrown something together.

TIA: But, I followed the formula. Those films make tons of money.

ROBIN: The ones that get made are just the tip of the iceberg. The vast majority go straight to the shredder.

        Your talents are wasted on this, Tia. Show me your Nyeri script.

TIA: It's not ready.

ROBIN: See? When it's something you actually have passion for, you take your time with it. You commit to it. That's what I want to read.

TIA: Okay. Thanks, Robin.

ROBIN: I'll probably enjoy it more than what Maurice Gilder has come up with.

TIA: I was hoping that I could read his version of the visit, actually. For context.

ROBIN: Here you go.

            She drops MAURICE's script on TIA's desk.

TIA: Seriously?

ROBIN: He dropped it off just before the power cut.

            The power comes back on.

TIA: Yes!

ROBIN: I'll need you to retype it and email it to me as a PDF as soon as you can.

TIA: We have the casting session this afternoon.

ROBIN: Right.

TIA: I can get started.

ROBIN: You're the best.

            TIA types. ROBIN exits. TIA picks up her script.

            It's not so bad.

            She begins to read. MAN and WOMAN enter.

MAN: Do you know where I might find a guy named Alex MacNeil?

WOMAN: I do, actually.

MAN: Well, good. Can't wait to give him a piece of mind.

WOMAN: Why's that?

MAN: He rejected my drawings. Doesn't have a clue what makes a good sailboat.

WOMAN: Oh. Well, my name is Alexandra.

MAN: Pleased to meet you.

WOMAN: Alexandra MacNeil.

MAN: Oh!

WOMAN: And you must be Christian Ramsay.

MAN: Guilty as charged.

WOMAN: I know more about sailboats than you think.

MAN: Have I lost myself a job?

WOMAN: It doesn't look good.

MAN: Let me plead my case over lunch.

WOMAN: I don't know.

MAN: Anywhere you like.

WOMAN: Well, all right, Christian.

MAN: Call me Captain. Everyone does.

> *TIA stops reading.*

TIA: What was I thinking?

> *TIA drops the script in the bin labelled 'to shred' and sits at her computer. She begins transcribing MAURICE's script.*

Dense fog. Day. Gradually, we see that it's not fog, but clouds. Sound effect. Plane engine. Fade to exterior. A plane emerges. Below it is the lush green of Africa.

Nice.

> *TIA continues reading and typing.*

Act 1, Scene 7: Mercy under Pressure

> *1952. Restaurant. There is a standoff between FAITH and MERCY. MERCY holds an official-looking document.*

FAITH: You have to do it. Training is around the corner.

MERCY: I will tell Talbot the truth; that you forged my signature.

FAITH: But I could go to jail.

MERCY: Which is no less than you deserve.

FAITH: You don't mean that, Mama.

MERCY: Maybe you'll finally learn that everything cannot always go your way.

FAITH: I don't think that way.

MERCY: Then why have bedrooms been reserved for both of us in the staff quarters?

FAITH: (*Busted.*) Well, I've never been to a fancy place like Sagana.

MERCY: You'll have to clean up this mess all by yourself.

FAITH: But, as far as Mr. Talbot knows, you've agreed.

MERCY: I don't care.

FAITH: Then he'll think that you're another ignorant African who can't do business in the modern world.

MERCY: Damn you.

> *MONTAGUE enters.*

We are not serving supper yet.

FAITH: I asked you to wait.

MERCY: You know this man?

FAITH: This is Montague. He works with Mr. Talbot.

MONTAGUE: Mrs. Nyanjiru. You need to come with me.

MERCY: Just because you work for the English, don't think you can tell me what to do!

FAITH: I'm sorry, Montague. This is my fault.

MERCY: Do not apologize for me. There is nothing to apologize for. Get out of my restaurant.

FAITH: Mama, calm down.

MERCY: Go home. We can't take advantage of Mrs. Otieno.

MONTAGUE: I just spoke with Mrs. Otieno.

MERCY: What? How do you know her?

MONTAGUE: She called to the telephone across the street. I'm sorry to say that your husband is in the hospital.

FAITH: Did he have another stroke?

MONTAGUE: All I know is that it is very serious.

> *FAITH embraces MERCY. MERCY is in shock.
> MONTAGUE helps her into a chair.*

MERCY: He was doing so well.

FAITH: He will be all right, Mama.

MONTAGUE: Help me take her to the car.

MERCY: Put the food in the icebox.

FAITH: It doesn't matter, Mama.

MERCY: And let it go to waste? I'll do it if you won't.

FAITH: No, I'm going.

FAITH goes to the kitchen.

MONTAGUE: Can I help you?

MERCY: Do you have a pen?

MONTAGUE: Yes.

> *He gives it to her. She begins to write on the back of one of the official papers.*

That is your itinerary.

MERCY: People need to know that we are closed until further notice.

MONTAGUE: I understand.

MERCY: If he dies, would Mr. Talbot hold me to my contract?

MONTAGUE: There is no need to think about that right now.

> *By now, she has put the note in the window.*

MERCY: When I think of all the times I wanted to be close enough to one of those English to give them a piece of my mind or to…

MONTAGUE: To what?

MERCY: I wonder what Dedan Kimathi would do if the Princess was so close to him.

MONTAGUE: That man is an enemy to the government.

MERCY: It would be my honour to help him take down the English.

MONTAGUE: Mrs. Nyanjiru!

MERCY: What?

MONTAGUE: I will pretend that I did not hear these things.

MERCY: Traitor.

MONTAGUE: I am not a traitor.

> *FAITH enters.*

FAITH: All right. Everything is put away.

MERCY: Thank you, dear.

MONTAGUE: Mrs. Nyanjiru…

MERCY: Thank you for the drive… and the pen.

> *She gives him the pen and goes to the door. FAITH puts her arm around her. MONTAGUE hasn't moved.*

FAITH: Montague?

MONTAGUE: Yes. I will get us there quickly.

> *They exit.*

Talbot (Geoffrey Pounsett) briefs Princess Elizabeth (Amanda Lisman).

Montague (Tony Ofori) delivers bad news to Mercy (Marcia Johnson) and Faith (Allison Edwards-Crewe).

Act 1, Scene 8: Casting

> *An undisclosed area. ELIZABETH sits, addressing the Commonwealth.*

ELIZABETH: For my twenty-first birthday, I welcome the opportunity to speak to all the peoples of the British Commonwealth Empire, wherever they live, whatever race they come from and whatever language they speak. I declare before you all that my whole life, whether it be long or short, shall be devoted to your service and to the service of our great imperial family to which we all belong. But I shall not have strength to carry out this resolution alone unless you join in it with me as I now invite you to do. I know that your support will be unfailingly given. God help me to make good my vow. And God bless all of you who are willing to share in it.

> *She gives a meaningful look. It's a beautiful moment which is then shattered by the sound of a very modern cell phone ringtone.*

TIA: (*From off.*) Sorry!

> *It's revealed that we're in 2015 and that Elizabeth is actually an actor (ASHLEY) auditioning to play her.*

ASHLEY: (*Different English accent.*) Couldn't have timed it better, though.

TIA: (*Entering.*) Sorry.

PATRICIA: Very nice, Ashley.

ASHLEY: Can I do it again? I can be more posh.

PATRICIA: No need. You sounded just like her.

ASHLEY: Really?

PATRICIA: Really. I'll call your agent as soon as I know. Tia will show you out.

                And Tia?

TIA: Yeah?

PATRICIA: Turn off your phone.

TIA: Sorry. (*To ASHLEY, as they exit.*) You were awesome.

ASHLEY: Let's hope so. I paid a dialect coach half a month's rent!

                TIA and ASHLEY leave. PATRICIA is on a headset.

PATRICIA: What did you think? Yeah, I agree. She's the one. Gilder shouldn't have any complaints. I like her even better than the silly cow we cast in the first place.

                TIA returns.

TIA: Are you ready?

PATRICIA: Yeah, we'll just bring them in one after the other.

TIA: Sure.

                TIA leaves.

PATRICIA: (*On phone.*) All right, moving on. See you tonight.

                PATRICIA takes off the headset, does a bit of stretching, then takes her place at the table. TIA re-enters with STEVE. She hands his photo and résumé to PATRICIA.

                Steven Edison.

STEVE: Steve. Hi.

PATRICIA: Nice to meet you.

STEVE: Thanks. So, there are no pages?

PATRICIA: Just going to ask you to improv a scenario.

STEVE: Improv?

PATRICIA: Yeah, I'll talk you through it.

STEVE: Which accent did you want?

PATRICIA: Doesn't matter. Tia, you'll be standing in for Elizabeth.

TIA: Cool. Okay.

PATRICIA: And Steven, if you could just take your spot there.

STEVE: Sure.

PATRICIA: Tia, you'll walk over to that box and stand on top of it. Steve, you'll be watching her every move. It'll just be easier if we shoot while the two of you follow my direction. Camera ready! Tia, just go back to that starting spot. Steve, the camera will be on you for this whole thing.

STEVE: Got it.

              TIA and STEVE follow PATRICIA's directions throughout.

PATRICIA: And action. Tia, start walking toward the box.

Steve, you're looking at her with a mix of admiration and empathy. That's right. You're really sad because she's really sad. Now she's at the top step, Tia. This is a tremendous moment. You feel that you have to do something. You want to say something but she doesn't understand your language. Good Steve, good. The emotion is building in you.

She's just standing there. What can you do to show how much you value her service and how sad you feel for her? Suddenly, you know what to do. You go directly to her. Go, Steve. That's it. Right. Now drop to your knees. Drop to your knees! Good. Good. And...kiss her feet.

TIA / STEVE: What?

PATRICIA: Keep rolling. Kiss her feet! Do it.

> *STEVE reluctantly kisses the tops of TIA's shoes.*

Good. Now stand. Go back to your position. And feel confident that your Sovereign knows that you are a loyal subject.

> *STEVE bows his head. He seems to be in disbelief.*

Good. You can't believe that you just did that. Nice touch, Steve. And cut! Thank you very much.

STEVE: Mm, yeah. You're welcome.

PATRICIA: We'll be contacting agents next week. If you get the part, you'll need to get immunized. Will that be problem?

STEVE: No, I don't think so.

PATRICIA: And your passport's up to date?

STEVE: Uh, yeah.

PATRICIA: Good. Tia will see you out. Tia, you can bring in the next one.

TIA: Okay.

> *Both TIA and STEVE leave in a daze. PATRICIA prepares herself for the next actor.*

Act 2, Scene 1: After the Funeral

> *1952. The empty restaurant. TALBOT is holding a bouquet of flowers at the door.*

TALBOT: Hello. Hello?

> *MERCY enters from the kitchen, wiping her hands. She wears an apron over her black dress.*

MERCY: Please come in, Mr. Talbot.

TALBOT: Are you sure?

MERCY: Yes, I could use a break.

> *He gives her the flowers.*

TALBOT: Just a token.

MERCY: Very thoughtful. Were you at the funeral?

TALBOT: No. I didn't think that it would be appropriate.

MERCY: You would have enjoyed it.

TALBOT: Enjoyed it?

MERCY: We remember our loved ones by celebrating in public and mourning in private.

TALBOT: That sounds wonderful.

MERCY: Please sit.

TALBOT: Thank you.

> *He sits. She joins him.*

MERCY: Would you like something to eat? There is more than enough *maharagwe*.

TALBOT: It is a kind offer but I am only here for a few minutes.

MERCY: I see.

TALBOT: You did the cooking for the guests?

MERCY: It is better to remain occupied in times such as this.

TALBOT: You are an admirable woman.

MERCY: You want to know if I will still cook for the princess.

TALBOT: I wouldn't dream of bringing up business matters at such a time.

                       She gives him a look.

              But the royal couple will be here in just over a week and we didn't approach anyone else.

MERCY: Why not?

TALBOT: We have a signed agreement with you.

MERCY: You should not put so much stock into that signature.

TALBOT: And perpetuate the unfortunate history between the English and Africa? No. Times are changing, Mrs. Nyanjiru.

MERCY: That contract is not valid, Mr. Talbot.

TALBOT: That is true.

MERCY: So, you know.

TALBOT: The delay does nullify it but we're overlooking that technicality. It was only fair to allow you a time of mourning.

MERCY: —

TALBOT: The ball is entirely in your court.

MERCY: It has never been this way for me.

TALBOT: I am sorry for that.

MERCY: Is there enough time for all the training?

TALBOT: I feel confident that you could manage in the time we have left.

MERCY: And you will reduce the fee, of course.

TALBOT: No, the amount we agreed upon stands.

MERCY: Are you really such a good man?

TALBOT: I try to be.

MERCY: I wish more English people were like you.

TALBOT: There are more of us than you think.

MERCY: Will you tell them to speak up?

TALBOT: Every chance I get.

MERCY: I will do it.

TALBOT: You will?

MERCY: I honour my contracts.

TALBOT: Thank you so much. I can't tell you what a relief – Once you meet Their Royal Highnesses, I am sure that you will be charmed by them.

MERCY: It is not my place to be charmed by them. It is my place to serve them.

TALBOT: As long as you feel that you won't let the unpleasantness from the past get in the way.

MERCY: I will do my job.

TALBOT: I believe that you will.

He hands her an envelope.

Here's an updated itinerary for you and Faith. My driver will take you to the Lodge on Monday afternoon.

MERCY: Montague.

TALBOT: Yes. I understand that he drove you and Faith to the hospital.

MERCY: It was very kind of him.

A crash from the kitchen.

I must help my daughter clean up.

TALBOT: Yes, it sounds like she could use a hand.

MERCY: Thank you for allowing her to come with me.

TALBOT: Well, I'm sure that the two of you will want to spend as much time together as you can for the next while.

MERCY: Yes. That is true.

Another crash.

TALBOT: Oh dear.

MERCY: She will be much more careful at the Lodge.

TALBOT: Yes, well... Good day.

MERCY: Good day.

TALBOT: And, again, my sincerest condolences.

MERCY: Thank you, Mr. Talbot.

TALBOT: Comportment lessons begin after your fittings on Monday.

MERCY: Yes.

> *TALBOT leaves.*

Can't have us swinging from the trees.

> *One last crash as MERCY walks to the kitchen with the flowers.*

Act 2, Scene 2: Tia's Awakening

> *2015. Production office. ROBIN and TIA are packing up the office.*

ROBIN: Hey, it's Tuesday. Where's your *Hello!* magazine?

TIA: Didn't get one.

ROBIN: What?

TIA: I'm just not interested these days.

ROBIN: Why not?

TIA: Don't believe in fairy tales anymore, I guess.

ROBIN: Does this have anything to do with the Kenya episode?

TIA: Did you read it?

ROBIN: Last night.

TIA: What did you think?

ROBIN: Colonialism at its finest.

TIA: I knew about the foot-kissing scene from the audition but...wow. Just, wow.

ROBIN: Yeah. Very disappointing.

TIA: All those years dressing up like princesses and waking up early for the royal wedding.

ROBIN: This would be the perfect time to work on your Nyeri script. I do my best writing when I'm worked up.

TIA: You're a writer?

ROBIN: I feel like I have to be. I'm not seeing myself represented enough on screen.

TIA: Are you kidding?

                ROBIN gives her a knowing look.

                Oh, right. What are you writing about?

ROBIN: Promise you won't tell anyone?

TIA: Promise.

ROBIN: It's a series set during the passing of the gross
                indecency laws. Did you know that they only
                applied to men?

TIA: No. When was this?

ROBIN: 1885. Queen Victoria thought that lesbians were
                a myth.

TIA: Get out!

ROBIN: So, while gay men were doing hard labour for
                their "crimes," certain women were setting up
                house together.

TIA: That's awesome!

ROBIN: It's what's keeping me going.

TIA: I'd love to read whatever you've got so far.

ROBIN: (*Pointing to her head.*) It's all up here for the time
                being. How's your script coming along?

TIA: I'm rewriting it. Gilder's script inspired me to go
                in another direction.

ROBIN: Intriguing.

TIA: Do you have anything else for me today?

ROBIN: No, remarkably.

TIA: Can I go early?

ROBIN: I'd say you earned it. Come to think of it, so have I.

TIA: Great.

ROBIN: Why don't we go for a drink? My treat.

TIA: Oh, thanks, but I can't.

ROBIN: Look, I wasn't coming on to you.

TIA: I know.

ROBIN: 'Cause you know I'm in a relationship.

TIA: I met her. Remember?

ROBIN: Oh, yeah.

TIA: Another time?

ROBIN: Sounds good.

                TIA puts on lipstick.

            Tia!

TIA: What?

ROBIN: Do you have a date?!

TIA: Just drinks.

ROBIN: Where would you find time to meet anyone?

TIA: I helped Casting, remember?

ROBIN: An actor, really?

                They begin their exit.

TIA: He's already kissed me.

Act 2, Scene 3: Comportment Lessons

> *1952. Sagana Lodge. TALBOT is sitting at a dining room table. A table setting is in front of him but there is no food. He waits.*

TALBOT: Faith.

FAITH: (*From off.*) Now?

TALBOT: Yes, as soon as she places her fork on her plate.

FAITH: (*From off.*) All right. Sorry.

TALBOT: It's why we practise. I'll go again. Ready?

FAITH: (*From off.*) Yes, Mr. Talbot.

> *TALBOT places the fork on the plate. FAITH enters. She curtsies stiffly and removes the plate from the right.*

TALBOT: From the left.

FAITH: *Kamae!* Sorry.

> *She removes the plate from the left, curtsies again and leaves. TALBOT looks exasperated.*

TALBOT: All right. Come on out.

> *FAITH returns with the dishes and puts them back on the table.*

FAITH: I'm so sorry, Mr. Talbot.

TALBOT: Remember, serve the *lady* from the *left*. "L" "L."

FAITH: Oh, yes. That's helpful. Thank you.

TALBOT: Now, let's have a look at that curtsy again.

>   *FAITH curtsies as she did before. She bows her head and waits.*

You're not being knighted.

Let me show you. (*He does.*) Place your right foot behind your left leg and bend your left knee and finish with a slight nod of the head. Give it a try.

>   *FAITH does a perfect curtsy.*

Well done.

FAITH: Thank you.

TALBOT: I expected to see your mother today.

FAITH: She had to settle some of my father's affairs.

TALBOT: I had hoped that she would get familiar with the kitchen.

FAITH: Don't worry. My mother can cook on any stove. I'll show her how to curtsy when I get home.

TALBOT: You have a room here.

FAITH: Monta – Mr. Mwangi will be driving me home tonight and pick us both up in the morning and we will move into our rooms.

TALBOT: My stomach is in knots right now.

FAITH: She will catch up. I promise.

TALBOT: It is so important that things go well.

FAITH: They will. Please take a seat, Your Royal Highness.

TALBOT: Oh, I'm not to be addressed –

FAITH pulls out the chair for him.

FAITH: Your Highness?

TALBOT: Oh, I see. Good. We'll give it one more try and call it a day.

FAITH: And I'll remember. "Lady from the left."

                He sits and FAITH pushes in the chair before giving a perfect curtsy.

TALBOT: Well done.

                FAITH exits. After a moment, TALBOT picks up the fork, puts it to his mouth and then rests it on the plate. He waits. She doesn't appear. He emits a deep, profound sigh.

Act 2, Scene 4: A Better Kiss

> *2015. A pub in London. STEVE and TIA are on a date.*

STEVE: Do you think you'll stay here?

TIA: It's tempting.

STEVE: London's a great city.

TIA: I love it. Have you ever been to Canada?

STEVE: No. Been to the States, though. My best mate was doing a show on Broadway.

TIA: Love New York.

STEVE: Came at the end of the run. We hired a car.

TIA: You were so close to Toronto!

STEVE: We thought about going there but we decided to do a Rocky instead.

TIA: Do a what?

STEVE: A Rocky. In Philadelphia. The Museum of Art?

TIA: Oh, you mean Rocky Balboa when he ran up the steps?

STEVE: Yeah.

TIA: That's a thing?

STEVE: We weren't the only ones.

> *TIA begins to laugh.*

Why are you laughing? It's a great movie.

TIA: I'm sorry.

STEVE: Here I thought that Canadians were so polite.

TIA: Not polite. Apologetic.

STEVE: Go on then.

TIA: I'm sorry for laughing.

STEVE: Thank you. Philadelphia's not so far from Toronto. You should try it.

TIA: I had been thinking of going to the Grand Canyon.

STEVE: I want to do that as well.

TIA: Will you do a Thelma and Louise?

STEVE: So very cold.

TIA: But I'm cute, right?

            They kiss for the first time.

            That was nice.

STEVE: A sight better than kissing your feet.

TIA: I was as surprised as you were.

STEVE: I could tell.

TIA: Do you think it really happened that way?

STEVE: The writer wouldn't fabricate something like that, would he?

TIA: I should look it up.

STEVE: Nothing to be done about it now.

TIA: I warned all the other guys after you.

STEVE: That was decent of you.

TIA: One of them refused to audition. Patricia didn't bat an eye. Just told him she understood and marked him down as unavailable.

Patricia directs Steve (Tony Ofori) in an audition with Tia (Allison Edwards-Crewe).

Tia (Allison Edwards-Crewe) and Steve (Tony Ofori) grab a few drinks.

STEVE: Good on her.

TIA: I feel like I'm supposed to say something about it before we go to camera.

STEVE: To…

TIA: The writer.

STEVE: You think that you can get Maurice Gilder to do rewrites?

TIA: Someone should!

STEVE: Oh, yeah. Go to his mansion in Ascot with your suggestions. I'm sure he'd welcome you with open arms.

TIA: Like I have anything resembling free time.

STEVE: Just as well, then.

TIA: Yeah.

A moment.

STEVE: Well, I booked a film.

TIA: Congratulations! What is it?

STEVE: Untitled American spy drama. I play a Secret Service agent.

TIA: Let's hear your accent.

STEVE: "This way, Mr. President. Your car is waiting."

TIA: It's like you're from the Midwest.

STEVE: Thanks.

TIA: When do you shoot?

STEVE: In about two weeks. It's a bigger part so my agent took me out of the running for your show.

TIA: Would you have done it otherwise?

STEVE: Free trip to Africa!

TIA: There's that.

STEVE: Might have taken the opportunity to find my
            roots. You already know yours, yeah?

TIA: Sure.

STEVE: Am I boring you?

TIA: What? No!

STEVE: You were thinking about the Kenya script again.

TIA: I was wondering how far Ascot is.

STEVE: All right, now. Steady on.

TIA: It was your idea.

STEVE: It was most definitely not!

TIA: I should have thought of it myself.

STEVE: Tia, don't do anything crazy.

TIA: Define crazy.

STEVE: Look, you're an unpaid intern. Just keep your
            head down.

TIA: All right. All right.

            She ponders.

STEVE: You're not going to let it go, are you?

TIA: (*Not convincingly.*) Sure.

STEVE: Tia.

            She kisses him.

TIA: What?

STEVE: Nothing.

They kiss.

Act 2, Scene 5: The Princess Arrives

> *1952. Sagana Lodge. TALBOT is checking for dust. MERCY enters. She is wearing a crisp white uniform.*

TALBOT: Mrs. Nyanjiru.

MERCY: Mr. Talbot.

TALBOT: I believe that there was an apron.

MERCY: One of the maids is ironing it.

TALBOT: Ah yes. Everything has to be just so.

MERCY: We have had several drills on how to line up when they arrive.

TALBOT: Good.

MERCY: Yes.

> *A moment.*

TALBOT: May I see it?

MERCY: What? Oh.

> *MERCY curtsies.*

TALBOT: Very good.

MERCY: It is not difficult.

TALBOT: One less thing to worry about.

MERCY: Everything is in place.

TALBOT: Except for the wild creature on the loose in the gardens.

MERCY: Wild creature?

> *MONTAGUE enters.*

TALBOT: Ah, Montague.

MONTAGUE: The Rolls is washed and the tank filled with petrol.

TALBOT: Very good.

FAITH enters, also in uniform.

FAITH: Hello, Mr. Talbot.

TALBOT: Faith.

FAITH: Mr. Mwangi.

MONTAGUE: Miss Nyanjiru.

FAITH: Will they be here soon?

TALBOT: There has been a slight delay. More well-wishers than expected along the road.

FAITH: I have been listening on the wireless. I cannot wait to see them in person.

TALBOT: Your enthusiasm is just the thing.

MERCY: Excuse me. I will see if my apron is ready.

TALBOT: Yes. Good.

MERCY exits.

I will check the grounds one last time.

MONTAGUE: They caught the mongoose.

TALBOT: Thank heavens. The thing was terrifying.

TALBOT exits.

MONTAGUE: How are you?

FAITH: Happy to be here. It is so sad at home without him.

MONTAGUE: You are bearing up quite well. As is your mother.

FAITH: What choice do we have?

MONTAGUE: She said some disturbing things the day that we went to the hospital.

FAITH: What things?

MONTAGUE: About taking down the English.

FAITH: She always talks about that.

MONTAGUE: I find it worrisome.

FAITH: You think that my mother would harm the princess?

MONTAGUE: She sounded like she wanted to.

FAITH: She probably doesn't even remember what she said.

MONTAGUE: I hope that you are right.

FAITH: You haven't said anything about my uniform. It's nicer than any dress I own.

MONTAGUE: It's lovely. Will you be able to keep it?

FAITH: No. I asked.

MONTAGUE: Shame.

FAITH: Will we be able to go for another drive soon?

MONTAGUE: Not while the royal couple is here. I am at the ready should anything happen to their regular driver.

FAITH: I could slip something into his food if you like.

MONTAGUE: Don't even joke about that, Faith.

FAITH: You are so serious when Mr. Talbot is around.

MONTAGUE: I could get a promotion when this is all over.

FAITH: You would move to England?

MONTAGUE: Maybe.

FAITH: Oh.

MONTAGUE: But not right away.

FAITH: Good.

MONTAGUE: You can get a seamstress to make a similar dress for you.

FAITH: What a wonderful idea.

> *Are they going to kiss? TALBOT enters breathlessly.*

TALBOT: They are moments away! Positions, everyone!

MONTAGUE: I will fetch Mrs. Nyanjiru.

FAITH: See you out there.

> *FAITH rushes outside. TALBOT adjusts flowers in a vase. MONTAGUE re-enters with MERCY whose uniform now includes an apron.*

TALBOT: Splendid.

> *There are the sounds of cheers and applause from outside. They compose themselves and exit.*

Act 2, Scene 6: Meeting Maurice

> *2015, a very posh living room in Ascot, England. TIA is taking in its opulence and beauty. She is wearing a dress that looks exactly like FAITH's uniform without the apron. There is lightning and a loud clap of thunder which makes her jump. MAURICE enters with two towels and hands one to her.*

TIA: Thank you.

> *She dries off from the rain while he drapes the other towel on the seat of an armchair.*

MAURICE: Not at all. That was quite the drenching.

TIA: And just from the sidewalk to your front door.

MAURICE: My apologies for there not being room for your friend to drop you closer.

TIA: I thought that maybe you had company.

MAURICE: No, just me and Sylvia.

TIA: Your wife?

MAURICE: My housekeeper.

TIA: Those cars all belong to you?

MAURICE: Just three of them. One belongs to Sylvia.

TIA: The Civic?

MAURICE: Yes. I don't usually have them all in the drive but we're tiling the garage.

TIA: Oh, my parents did that too. Did you get the interlocking rubber ones?

MAURICE: Porcelain, actually.

TIA: I've never heard of using porcelain tiles for a garage.

MAURICE: Found them in Italy. Quite durable, apparently.

                MAURICE takes the towel from her and drapes it over the fireplace screen. He tends to his drink cart.

TIA: I can't thank you enough, Mr. Gilder. I've never interviewed a celebrity before.

MAURICE: Well, I wouldn't call myself a celebrity.

TIA: You won an Oscar!

MAURICE: Probably out of pity after three nominations.

TIA: Oh, no. You deserved it.

MAURICE: You're very kind.

TIA: Look at all those theatre awards.

MAURICE: You're an aspiring playwright yourself?

TIA: Screenwriter and showrunner.

                He has two drinks and offers one to her.

MAURICE: Here you are.

TIA: Not for me, thanks.

MAURICE: Nonsense. You must be chilled to the bone. This is as good as a hot water bottle.

TIA: Well, thank you.

                She takes the drink and puts it on the side table before sitting on the towel-draped chair.

MAURICE: Jumping right over theatre, are you?

TIA: I guess so.

MAURICE: In my day, everyone started in theatre.

TIA: Some people still do.

MAURICE: So, you're at school and you have a job on the series.

TIA: I'm an intern.

MAURICE: A dogsbody then.

TIA: A dog's body?

MAURICE: Shakespearean turn of phrase. Someone who does all the unwanted menial jobs.

TIA: Sounds about right.

MAURICE: You were at the shops when I visited the office. What else do they have you doing?

TIA: Paperwork mainly. I copied all the scripts and had them couriered.

MAURICE: I received mine safe and sound. Good job.

TIA: Thanks. By the way, I've read all ten episodes.

MAURICE: Goodness.

TIA: You're a wonderful writer.

MAURICE: Thank you, my dear.

TIA: The characters jump off the page.

MAURICE: Caress the divine detail, as they say.

TIA: Nabokov.

MAURICE: They're teaching you well in that program.

TIA: I'm learning more from being in the production office. And we start shooting tomorrow!

MAURICE: It's like Christmas holiday.

TIA: I don't want to take up too much of your time.

MAURICE: I am at your service.

TIA: Can you tell me how writing this series is different from writing a play?

MAURICE: Well, there's a damn sight more money involved.

TIA: I'm sure.

MAURICE: In a nutshell, it's more visual. A ten-second flashback can replace pages of dialogue.

                  On occasion, the director will make those changes without even bothering to bloody well consult with the writer. My apologies.

TIA: For what?

MAURICE: Oh, that's right. "Bloody" means nothing in America.

TIA: I'm Canadian.

MAURICE: What brings you here?

TIA: Film school.

                  TIA takes a notebook and pen from her bag and begins writing.

MAURICE: Don't they have film schools in Canada?

TIA: They were a little too close to home.

MAURICE: On a grand adventure, are you?

TIA: It's nice being able to go to Paris for the weekend. Not that I have time these days.

MAURICE: I'm impressed by your work ethic.

TIA: Thanks. I'd like to talk about the research that you did.

MAURICE: Someone else was tasked with that but I already had quite a bit of knowledge about the queen.

TIA: I thought that I did too, but I really learned a lot about her from your scripts.

MAURICE: She's a fascinating woman.

TIA: You taught me a lot about Churchill too.

MAURICE: I was even more familiar with him.

TIA: You're a fan?

MAURICE: I went to St. George's here in Ascot. He is our most famous old boy.

TIA: What a coincidence.

MAURICE: I feel that I was born to write this series.

TIA: Write what you know?

MAURICE: Indeed.

TIA: I've always wanted to add to that saying. Never mind.

MAURICE: No. Tell me.

TIA: "Write what you know. Research what you don't."

MAURICE: You are clever.

TIA: Thank you. I really liked the character of Churchill's junior secretary. And her roommate.

MAURICE: Thank you. I'm fond of those characters as well.

TIA: I like how you juxtaposed their lives alongside the lives of the royals and the government elite.

MAURICE: Thank you, my dear.

TIA: I loved how she started off terrified of him.

MAURICE: I would say starstruck.

TIA: Okay. She was in the Kenya episode, which was intriguing.

MAURICE: Yes.

TIA: Even with its obvious problems.

MAURICE: I beg your pardon?

TIA: There definitely wasn't much research done about the key figures in Kenya.

MAURICE: Euen Mitchell was quite the character but – .

TIA: He was the white governor in the newsreels.

MAURICE: Yes. I toyed with giving him a larger role.

TIA: There were also hundreds of tribal leaders in that footage.

MAURICE: Pity there was no sound.

TIA: Mitchell introduced the couple to some of the chiefs.

MAURICE: Just glad-handing, really.

TIA: Why didn't Dedan Kimathi make it onto the character list?

Thunder. Flickering of lights.

MAURICE: Not familiar with him.

TIA: He was one of the leaders of the Mau Mau Uprising.

MAURICE: That didn't happen during the royal visit.

TIA: There were stirrings.

MAURICE: The rebellion didn't come into full force until months later.

TIA: Some say that the trip was one of its triggers.

MAURICE: Yes, well, that wasn't the focus of the episode.

TIA: No, it wasn't.

MAURICE: Listen –

TIA: Just a few more questions. I'm learning so much!

MAURICE: Yes, well…

TIA: So, the impression I'm getting is that you had a lot of history to sort through before you could decide what would make good drama.

MAURICE: I would say that that is a fair statement.

TIA: And you do.

MAURICE: I do what?

TIA: Make good drama.

MAURICE: Thank you, my dear. The secret to –

TIA: What about Mercy and Faith Nyanjiru?

MAURICE: Who were they?

TIA: They worked at Sagana Lodge during the visit.

MAURICE: Why would I know the names of the staff?

TIA: That's true. Kitchen staff don't tend to make it into history books.

MAURICE: I'm beginning to suspect –

TIA: Except maybe Sirhan Sirhan.

Thunder. Flickering of lights.

MAURICE: Excuse me?

TIA: He killed Bobby Kennedy.

MAURICE: Well, actually Sirhan wasn't kitchen staff.

TIA: Whatever. Did you come across the name Montague Mwangi?

MAURICE: I don't believe so.

TIA: He worked for the British government in Kenya.

MAURICE: How did you find all of this...I'm sorry. I've forgotten your name.

TIA: Tia.

MAURICE: As in a Spanish aunt?

TIA: In Kiswahili, it means respect. My last name means psychic power.

MAURICE: What is it?

TIA: My psychic power?

MAURICE: No, your name.

TIA: Mwangi.

MAURICE: Is it a coincidence that you have the same last name as that Montague fellow?

TIA: No, it isn't.

MAURICE: This isn't just a student interview, is it?

TIA: Well, I am a student. And this is an interview.

MAURICE: You are here under false pretenses. You can leave now.

TIA: Mr. Gilder, you're making a terrible mistake with this episode.

MAURICE: I'll be sure to mention this to Robin.

TIA: She has no idea that I was coming. Mr. Gilder, I just –

MAURICE: I don't want to call the authorities, but I will.

                She's about to protest. He picks up the phone.

TIA: I'll just text my friend to come get me.

MAURICE: Do that.

                MAURICE puts the phone down. TIA sends a text. After a few moments, she receives a notification. She reads it and puts her phone away.

TIA: He's on his way.

MAURICE: Good.

                He pours himself a stiff drink. Thunder. Flickering of lights. A long, awkward moment.

TIA: I'd like you to consider that maybe you have an unconscious bias.

MAURICE: Well, who doesn't, you silly girl. It's called unconscious, after all.

TIA: You've got me there.

MAURICE: At least you didn't say "privilege."

TIA: How much do Italian porcelain garage tiles cost?

MAURICE: You will not make me feel guilty. I worked hard for all of this. And I worked damned hard on that script. I'm exceedingly proud of it. You swan in here and say: "change this" and "change that." Who do you think you are? I'm a bloody good writer.

                He takes a big swig from his glass.

TIA: Then it shouldn't take much to fix your mistakes.

MAURICE: That's it. You can wait outside!

> *Thunder and lightning.*

TIA: In this weather?

MAURICE: I don't care if you drown.

TIA: Well, I suppose it's better than making me kiss your feet.

MAURICE: Now, see here – !

TIA: I looked everywhere. I couldn't find anything about anyone doing that.

MAURICE: I said that you can wait outside!

> *A tremendous series of lightning strikes and thunder rumbles happen. The lights go out and come back on.*

TIA: (*After a moment.*) Do you have an extra umbrella?

MAURICE: Go on. Sit down.

> *She does. She takes the drink from the side table and has a sip.*

You have no idea how difficult it is to be a dramatic writer in this day and age. Especially as a white man.

TIA: Please tell me.

MAURICE: Even if I had found out about the Kenyans you mentioned; if I'd given them dialogue, I'd be accused of cultural appropriation.

TIA: No danger of that in the current script.

MAURICE: I can't believe that I fell for that innocent act of yours.

TIA: And you made Elizabeth so perfect.

MAURICE: By all accounts, she is a highly devoted and even-tempered person.

TIA: And she could bestow you with your very own knighthood.

MAURICE: Not another word or you can wait out in the deluge.

TIA: OK. OK. (*Re: drink.*) This is really good.

MAURICE: Glad to win your approval on something.

TIA: Could you at least consider fleshing out a Black character?

MAURICE: There were no meaningful interactions between Elizabeth and the Africans.

TIA: There were pictures and newsreels of her meeting several Black people.

MAURICE: Not the Mau Mau leader.

TIA: What about that little boy with the bouquet?

MAURICE: What little boy?

TIA: His nickname was Prince because he was born the same day as Charles. He was on the tarmac.

MAURICE: Oh, yes. He held the flowers behind his back. She had to reach around him to get them.

TIA: Why not write a scene about his parents being told that their little boy had been selected to present flowers to the princess?

MAURICE: Riveting.

TIA: It can be.

MAURICE: Look, the episode may have been set in Kenya but the story was about the King's death, which happened in England. I can't devote time to minor characters when the bigger story needs to be told.

TIA: What about Churchill's junior secretary and her roommate? They were minor characters who got to be part of the bigger story.

MAURICE: –

TIA: Did you speak with their descendants? Is the roommate still alive?

MAURICE: You know damn well that neither of those women existed.

TIA: Yet they had a meaningful story arc.

MAURICE: The producers wanted me to write about the great fog. You try creating drama about a weather pattern.

TIA: You needed a human element. I get that.

MAURICE: That was a damn fine tragic moment with that lovely young girl getting lost in the fog.

TIA: You could have created Black characters in the same way.

MAURICE. Where's that friend of yours?

TIA: You gave Churchill a relationship with a secretary who didn't even exist. Why not do the same thing for Elizabeth with a cook or waitress?

MAURICE: Enough!

> *He pours himself another drink. She takes a sip from hers. They both sit in silence.*

(*Sighs.*) The cook and the waitress. What were their names again?

TIA: Really?

MAURICE: There was some concern that there aren't enough women in that episode. Not good enough that the bloody lead is female.

TIA: What do you want to know about them?

He picks up a notebook and pen.

MAURICE: Anything.

TIA: All right. Mercy Nyanjiru and her daughter Faith joined the staff at the Sagana Lodge for the royal visit. Faith met Montague Mwangi and they eventually got married.

There's a knock at the door.

MAURICE: Sylvia will let him in. You said that Mercy's last name was Nyanjiru?

TIA: Yes. Her daughter's name was Faith.

MAURICE: How old?

TIA: Twenty-one.

STEVE enters.

STEVE: Hey.

TIA: Hi. This is Steve.

MAURICE: Maurice Gilder.

STEVE: Hi. I've seen your plays.

MAURICE: Good. Thanks.

STEVE: It's really coming down.

TIA: We'd better get going then.

MAURICE: What?

TIA: It's a long drive.

STEVE: Especially in this weather.

MAURICE: You drop all kinds of hints for me to include your ancestors in the script and then you run off?

TIA: My great-grandparents were tea garden farmers. They never served the queen. And I have no idea who did.

MAURICE: You led me to believe –

TIA: I made them up.

MAURICE: You what?

TIA: Mercy. Faith. Even Montague. It was easy.

STEVE: Mwangi is the most common surname in Kenya.

MAURICE: Is it, now?

TIA: The junior secretary in your script got to represent a change in Churchill's mood. You could use Black characters to represent...

MAURICE: To represent what?

TIA: To...represent. That's it. Let someone talk to the princess about how colonialism affects them. Give them more to do than gaze at her adoringly or kiss her feet.

                STEVE has handed her a script, which she hands to MAURICE.

STEVE: Hot off the presses.

MAURICE: What's this?

TIA: Just a little something I threw together.

STEVE: Excuse me.

MAURICE: Excuse you?

TIA: He needs you to get out of the way.

MAURICE: Get out of the way of what?

He moves and STEVE drags his chair to another position.

TIA: What if Faith forged her mother's signature on the Sagana contract?

MAURICE: They weren't real people!

STEVE: Neither was Churchill's junior secretary and her roommate. (*To TIA.*) You already covered that, right?

TIA: Yeah. We're good. (*To MAURICE.*) If you tell a good story with believable, relatable characters, it won't matter if they were real people or not.

MAURICE: Are you really telling me how to write?

STEVE: She's just making suggestions.

TIA: (*To MAURICE.*) Mercy could have been one of the women who marched against the white settlers five years earlier in Murang'a. The idea of serving the monarchy could really rankle her.

MAURICE: But she takes the job anyway, according to you.

TIA: So that she could get close to the Princess.

MAURICE: And why would she do that if she was so opposed to the British?

TIA: The Lodge was isolated, so it would make sense that security was focused on the perimeter. Mercy could see this as an opportunity.

MAURICE: An opportunity for what?

STEVE: No spoilers, Tia.

TIA: I got excited.

STEVE: Great stakes, though.

TIA: Thanks.

> *TIA and STEVE are moving furniture around.
> (MERCY and ELIZABETH might even help.)
> Finally, we are back in Sagana Lodge. TIA and
> STEVE settle MAURICE in his own chair out
> of the way of the action.*

MAURICE: Where are we?

TIA: Sagana Lodge. Isn't it sweet?

MAURICE: A bit frilly.

TIA: This is just my version. You could make it more
             rustic.

MAURICE: I could, could I?

> *She puts on FAITH's apron. STEVE puts on
> MONTAGUE's jacket.*

TIA: I just wanted you to see that there's another
             approach that you can take.

STEVE: It's really brilliant.

TIA: Thanks, Steve.

> *She hands him her drink. He finishes it.*

STEVE: Mm. Smooth.

> *TIA and STEVE exit. MAURICE is left alone
> and perplexed in his new surroundings.*

Act 2, Scene 7: The World Changes

> *1952. Sagana Lodge. MERCY is looking over a despondent FAITH.*

FAITH: I served her from the right! You should have seen Mr. Talbot's face.

MERCY: He always looks like that.

FAITH: I won't be serving her again.

MERCY: Good. I need your help in the kitchen. The staff is so preoccupied.

FAITH: Mama, people like us don't get to meet people like them. Aren't you even a little bit... I don't know...

MERCY: Impressed?

FAITH: Yes.

MERCY: No.

FAITH: Both of them are very nice. And her eyes.

MERCY: What about them?

FAITH: They are a different kind of blue.

MERCY: You are falling under her spell.

FAITH: No, Mama. I just think that her eyes are pretty.

MERCY: She should not be leading this country. Pretty eyes or not.

FAITH: Mama, don't say things like that. That's why the regular chef isn't here. He's anti-monarchy and refused to cook for her.

MERCY: A true patriot. I shall give him some of the money I earn here.

FAITH: Not too much, please.

MERCY: Don't worry. You are going to school, my bright
                girl.

FAITH: I'm sorry, Mama.

MERCY: For?

FAITH: I could have tried harder to convince you instead
                of taking things into my own hands.

MERCY: You did try awfully hard.

FAITH: I'm sorry that I forged your –

MERCY: Shh. I understand why you did it.

FAITH: I promise that I will never do anything like that
                again.

MERCY: Good.

                She notices something under the table.

                What is that?

FAITH: (*Not paying attention.*) Hm?

MERCY: It is rat poison from when they were trying to
                trap the mongoose. I told you that the staff was
                preoccupied.

FAITH: Mm-hm.

                *MERCY sees that FAITH's focus is through the
                window. A thought comes to her. She sweeps
                up the rat poison into her handkerchief which
                she then puts into her apron pocket. She acts
                as though nothing has happened.*

MERCY: Would you like to walk in the gardens with me?
                There's a bridge. They say the fish almost dance
                on the water.

FAITH: Mm-hm.

MERCY: Oh, for goodness sake. Where is he?

FAITH: Who?

MERCY: Won't you join us, Montague?

> *After a moment, MONTAGUE makes his sheepish entrance.*

MONTAGUE: Hello, Mrs. Nyanjiru.

MERCY: Hello, Montague.

FAITH: Hello.

MONTAGUE: Hello.

MERCY: Montague, I never did thank you properly for that day.

MONTAGUE: No need. I only wish the outcome had been different.

FAITH: (*Changing the subject.*) Let us listen to some music.

> *She turns on the wireless and fiddles with the knob. The odd strain of music and talk is heard through tremendous static. An English male announcer's voice becomes clear. "…sad day… England… the colonies. …royal standard (static)… half mast. (static) Princess Elizabeth (static)…"*

MONTAGUE: Something has happened.

> *TALBOT runs into the room and turns off the wireless.*

TALBOT: Please keep the set turned off.

MONTAGUE: What is it, sir?

TALBOT: There is some news. We don't want the princess to find out on the wireless.

FAITH: (*Guessing.*) The King has died.

MERCY: Faith!

TALBOT: I'm afraid that she is right. Long live the Queen.

MONTAGUE: Oh, no.

TALBOT: We must endeavour to keep the news from her until the Duke returns.

FAITH: He won't be back until tomorrow.

TALBOT: I am going to fetch him now. Montague, we're taking the Rolls.

MERCY: I will cover the wireless.

FAITH: I will try to find the princess.

TALBOT: Good. Thank you.

> *FAITH exits.*

Mercy, if she comes here, keep her company!

MERCY: Me?

TALBOT: I'm counting on you. Distract her.

MERCY: I will bring ginger beer. She enjoyed it last night.

TALBOT: Yes. Good.

> *TALBOT and MONTAGUE exit. MERCY takes the lacy table cloth off the table and puts it on the wireless. She goes to the kitchen. After a moment, Princess ELIZABETH enters. She is wearing jeans and is carrying a pair of*

binoculars. She walks to the covered wireless out of curiosity. MERCY enters with a pitcher and glasses on a tray just as ELIZABETH is removing the cloth.

MERCY: No!

ELIZABETH: Goodness gracious!

MERCY: The wireless. It's dangerous!

ELIZABETH: What?

MERCY: It shocked the gardener. Burned his hand. He is having it attended to right now.

ELIZABETH: Good lord. Thank you so much for warning me.

ELIZABETH begins to leave.

MERCY: Would you like some ginger beer?

ELIZABETH: What a wonderful idea.

MERCY pulls out a chair.

I'll take it with me.

MERCY: To your room?

ELIZABETH: My, how inquisitive you are.

MERCY: The glass may slip from your hands. Because of your gloves. I can escort you to your room.

ELIZABETH: How very kind.

MERCY: Good.

ELIZABETH: You may escort me to the lounge in back.

MERCY: Yes, the view is very nice.

ELIZABETH: I saw some of the staff gathered around another set.

MERCY: They are listening to a Swahili program.

ELIZABETH: I distinctly heard English.

MERCY: Maybe they were trying to find their broadcast and something had come through from England.

ELIZABETH: I might be able to convince them to change it to the BBC.

MERCY: Stop!

> *ELIZABETH begins to leave again. MERCY blocks her path.*

ELIZABETH: What on Earth are you doing?

MERCY: This is my country, not yours!

ELIZABETH: It would serve you well to remember that I am your future Sovereign.

MERCY: What good does that do me?

ELIZABETH: A great deal, actually.

MERCY: Can you really be so blind?

ELIZABETH: Whatever your grievances, you cannot expect me to solve them this very moment.

MERCY: I expect you to at least hear them.

ELIZABETH: This is supposed to be my holiday.

MERCY: From what? Cutting ribbons? Receiving bouquets?

ELIZABETH: We have only tried to do good in this country.

MERCY: You took away our land that had passed from mother to daughter for generations. You paid us a pittance to work on it.

ELIZABETH: I did no such thing.

Tia (Allison Edwards-Crewe) interviews Maurice (Geoffrey Pounsett).

Amanda Lisman as Princess Elizabeth.

MERCY: I've waited my whole life to tell you people what
                I think of you.

ELIZABETH: This is neither the time nor place. Talbot!

MERCY: He is not here.

ELIZABETH: You shall be escorted off the premises.

MERCY: Then I will make the most of the few moments
                we have together.

                           MERCY sits.

ELIZABETH: You are not to sit in my presence.

MERCY: Sit if you are so offended.

ELIZABETH: I prefer to stand.

MERCY: Have it your way.

                           A moment.

                I was one of the protesters in the Murang'a
                women's revolt against the English white
                settlers.

ELIZABETH: I had nothing to do with that.

MERCY: Do you care about your subjects or not? Or do
                you want us to pretend that everything is fine in
                the Empire?

ELIZABETH: –

MERCY: Don't let me stop you from pretending.

                           *MERCY gestures for ELIZABETH to leave.
                           ELIZABETH contemplates leaving but decides
                           to stay.*

ELIZABETH: What was the focus of the revolt?

MERCY: After years of farming our ancestors' land for the white settlers the soil quality was failing rapidly. They told us to terrace the land to combat the erosion. We were expected to do this for no pay an extra two days per month. When we refused, they declared the Forced Labour Decree. In other words, slavery.

ELIZABETH: I knew nothing of this.

MERCY: We had more than enough to do at home, so we marched to the district headquarters. One hundred and fifty women. We were all arrested and fined. My husband and I were paying off the fine in modest installments as best as we could but then he fell ill. So instead of paying the fine, I paid for his treatment.

> *MERCY reaches into her apron pocket and drops the contents of her handkerchief into the pitcher without ELIZABETH noticing.*

Jacob was a healthy man. No one can tell me that his stroke was not brought on by all the strife.

ELIZABETH: I believe I will sit now.

> *ELIZABETH sits.*

I heard of your husband's passing. I am deeply sorry.

That must account for this shocking behaviour of yours. Talbot said that you are a woman of admirable character.

MERCY: Did he?

ELIZABETH: Yes. A glowing review. And your meals have been wonderful.

MERCY: Thank you.

ELIZABETH: And so recently after such a tragic loss. Please accept my sympathies.

Do you still owe fines?

MERCY: No. They garnisheed my wages, leaving us next to nothing to live on. We moved to Nyeri so that I could take over my brother-in-law's restaurant.

ELIZABETH: What a heartbreaking story.

MERCY: Ours is just one of many.

ELIZABETH: You were right to insist that I listen to you.

MERCY: I do not think that Mr. Talbot would agree.

ELIZABETH: It was refreshing to have someone speak so frankly to me. Like an ordinary woman.

MERCY: But you are not ordinary.

ELIZABETH: Can't we pretend for just a few moments more?

MERCY: Before you have me escorted from the premises?

ELIZABETH: Let us forget about that.

MERCY: –

ELIZABETH: I imagine that you are owed more than a few kindnesses.

MERCY: I had promised Talbot that I would not let the past get in the way of serving you.

ELIZABETH: It was a momentary lapse.

MERCY: Well... I thank you for understanding.

ELIZABETH: It is my duty.

MERCY: You will be a good queen.

ELIZABETH: I will do my very best.

MERCY: Will you change your name, the way that your
               father did?

ELIZABETH: It is not time to speak of such things. The King is
               still on the throne. Too ill to travel at the moment
               but he is very much on the mend. You know that
               he was never meant to be king.

MERCY: I remember.

ELIZABETH: He worked to bring together people of different
               classes when he was Duke of York. Did you ever
               hear of the Industrial Welfare Society?

MERCY: No.

ELIZABETH: Well, my father was its president. His goal was
               to bring worker and employer together. The
               Forced Labour Decree goes against everything
               that he believes in.

               I will tell the King your story when I get home.

MERCY: You would tell the King about me?

               *Shockingly, ELIZABETH begins to pour
               ginger beer into a glass.*

ELIZABETH: I will write a note to myself the moment that I
               get back to my room.

               *ELIZABETH slides a glass to MERCY and
               pours a glass for herself.*

MERCY: You are serving me?

ELIZABETH: It will be our secret.

               *MERCY is riveted. ELIZABETH takes off her
               gloves and picks up her glass.*

               Cheers.

               *MERCY picks up her glass. ELIZABETH raises
               her glass to her lips.*

MERCY: Wait!

> *She grabs the glass from her.*

ELIZABETH: My word!

MERCY: A big black spider!

ELIZABETH: Where?

MERCY: In your glass.

ELIZABETH: Let me see.

> *MERCY pours the contents of the glass out of the window.*

MERCY: There! See it crawling away?

ELIZABETH: No.

MERCY: It is gone now. Very fast.

ELIZABETH: One would think that it would have drowned.

MERCY: Must be very powerful. With strong poison.

ELIZABETH: Well, I thank you for your quick actions.

MERCY: You are most welcome. I will make some more.

ELIZABETH: I think I will be fine with water.

MERCY: Yes, I will get some.

> *MERCY starts to leave but then remembers that she can't leave the Princess.*

You know that Sagana means spider in my language.

ELIZABETH: No, I did not.

> *TALBOT enters.*

TALBOT: Your Royal Highness!

MERCY: (*Under her breath.*) Oh, thank God.

TALBOT: Ma'am. The Duke has arrived.

ELIZABETH: Oh, I did not expect him back today. I will change into a frock and meet him.

TALBOT: It is of no consequence. He is also wearing dungarees.

ELIZABETH: "Sauce for the goose." Thank you, Talbot.

TALBOT: He's on the bridge. A lovely spot.

He wipes at his eyes.

ELIZABETH: Are you all right?

TALBOT: I… I am…

MERCY: I found something that will help with your allergies, Mr. Talbot.

TALBOT: Oh? Yes, thank you so much, Mrs. Nyanjiru.

ELIZABETH: I shall be off then.

ELIZABETH waits. TALBOT clears his throat.

TALBOT: Mrs. Nyanjiru.

MERCY looks to him. He does a subtle curtsy. MERCY turns to ELIZABETH and offers her hand. ELIZABETH accepts and shakes her hand.

ELIZABETH: Thank you for our chat, Mercy. I shall never forget it.

MERCY: Thank you for your promise.

ELIZABETH leaves.

TALBOT: Why did you not curtsy?

MERCY: Because I did not want to.

TALBOT: You disappoint me, Mrs. Nyanjiru.

MERCY: I accept that.

TALBOT: Thank you for keeping the secret, in any case.

MERCY: It was not easy.

TALBOT: How were you able to fill the time?

MERCY: We just chatted. Woman to woman.

TALBOT: What the blazes?

MERCY: I feel bad for her. I know what it is to see a strong man deteriorate and then to lose him.

TALBOT: I hope you don't mind that I told her about your husband.

MERCY: It's good that you did. It made a difference.

TALBOT: It is an emotional day.

MERCY: Yes.

TALBOT: She did not want to leave England. I convinced her that he would be all right.

MERCY: You could not have known.

TALBOT: He was so frail at Heathrow.

MERCY: Do you think it is right that we are watching them?

TALBOT: If you can look away, you're made of stronger stuff than I am.

MERCY: He doesn't appear to be telling her right away.

TALBOT: She's probably asking him about his hunting trip. What a beautiful smile she has.

MERCY: Not for much longer.

TALBOT: No. The world changes today.

MERCY: The commonwealth of the future replacing the
                imperial past?

TALBOT: It is what I believe.

MERCY: I sincerely hope that you are right.

> *MERCY and TALBOT watch Philip and
> ELIZABETH. The announcement plays:
> "His Majesty, King George the Sixth, has
> died peacefully in his sleep at Sandringham
> House. The official announcement from
> Sandringham, given at 10:45 Greenwich
> Mean Time, said the King retired in his usual
> health, but passed away in his sleep and was
> found dead in bed at 7:30 by a servant. He
> was 56, and was known to have been suffering
> from a worsening lung condition. Princess
> Elizabeth, who is at the Royal Hunting Lodge
> in Kenya, immediately becomes Queen at the
> age of 25. She has been informed of her father's
> death and..."*

Epilogue

The announcement from the previous scene bleeds into the transition to this scene and then morphs into another announcement on June 23, 2016.

ANNOUNCER: (*Voiceover.*) The UK has voted to leave the European Union, shocking the world and revealing a divided country.

An apartment in London where there has been a celebration. STEVE and TIA are watching TV, stunned.

TIA: Why aren't you more upset?

STEVE: I've had time to get used to it.

TIA: Twenty-four hours?!

STEVE: The writing was on the wall long before that.

TIA: (*Re: the TV.*) There's that idiot again.

STEVE: I understand why you want the sound off when he's talking.

TIA: Just turn it off. All the way.

STEVE: Yes, ma'am.

TIA: You voted to stay, right?

STEVE: What? Of course I did.

TIA: Sorry.

STEVE: My apologetic Canadian.

There's a knock at the door.

TIA: A latecomer.

STEVE:　　　I'll go.

> *STEVE goes to the door. TIA tidies up a bit.*

(*From off.*) What a nice surprise.

PATRICIA:　(*From off.*) We're not too late, are we?

STEVE:　　　(*From off.*) Of course not. She'll be chuffed to see you.

ROBIN:　　　(*From off.*) We'll see about that.

> *ROBIN and PATRICIA enter.*

TIA:　　　　Patricia!

> *She gives her a warm hug.*

PATRICIA:　Sorry to be so late.

> *The atmosphere is suddenly chilly.*

TIA:　　　　Hi, Robin.

ROBIN:　　　Tia.

TIA:　　　　I can't believe that you're here.

ROBIN:　　　It's all thanks to Pat.

PATRICIA:　You said you'd be nice.

ROBIN:　　　Doesn't get much nicer than this.

> *She presents a very expensive bottle of champagne.*

STEVE:　　　Are you serious?

PATRICIA:　Robin's missed you more than she lets on.

STEVE:　　　Should we save it?

ROBIN: Pop the cork. It's good to have something to celebrate after yesterday.

STEVE: Right.

TIA: You called it about Brexit.

ROBIN: Doesn't make it any easier to swallow. Glad to be busy at work.

TIA: How's it going?

ROBIN: Finished principal photography.

TIA: Congratulations.

ROBIN: Five months 'til the premiere.

TIA: Hard to believe.

ROBIN: You were missed. Especially in Africa.

PATRICIA: Now you're just rubbing her nose in it.

TIA: It's all right.

PATRICIA: It was so beautiful there.

STEVE: Who played the foot-kisser?

PATRICIA: Excellent South African actor. He's toured five countries in his one-man show about Mandela.

TIA: You owe him.

PATRICIA: Too right.

ROBIN: He's not the only one owed something.

TIA: Robin, how many times do I have to tell you that I'm sorry?

ROBIN: It was a bloody stupid thing to do.

PATRICIA: The two of you should have it out. Steve?

STEVE: What?

PATRICIA: Let me help you with the champagne.

STEVE: I can do – Oh, right. This way to the kitchen.

                      They start to leave.

PATRICIA: Be nice.

                      PATRICIA and STEVE go to the kitchen.

ROBIN: You could have ruined your career before it even got started.

TIA: Someone had to say something.

ROBIN: Well, Gilder didn't change a single word of that script.

TIA: That's too bad.

ROBIN: So, it was all a waste of time.

TIA: I don't think so.

ROBIN: You're lucky that he didn't charge you with trespassing.

TIA: I was more worried that you'd get in trouble.

ROBIN: Too right. You hacked my email to set up that ridiculous meeting.

TIA: Well, not really hacked. You just left your account open.

ROBIN: Remarkable.

TIA: That's the only thing I feel bad about. That's why I quit.

ROBIN: Three days before we left for Africa.

TIA: I was making a statement. I thought you'd be proud of me.

ROBIN: It was unprofessional.

TIA: I wasn't being paid!

ROBIN: You know what I mean.

TIA: I'm sorry that I left you in the lurch and I'm sorry that I impersonated you. But I stand behind everything else.

ROBIN: I get it. I get it.

TIA: So, you forgive me?

ROBIN: Come here.

> *They hug. PATRICIA pokes her head around the door.*

PATRICIA: Go for it, Steve!

> *A champagne cork pops.*

ROBIN: What about your script?

TIA: I adapted it into a stage play.

> *STEVE and PATRICIA enter with glasses of champagne.*

STEVE: It's brilliant.

TIA: I'm trying to get it produced in Toronto.

ROBIN: You're leaving us?

TIA: My student visa's about to expire.

ROBIN: Just when we've made up.

PATRICIA: That's worth celebrating.

They all have their glasses.

STEVE: To Tia!

ALL: (*Except TIA.*) To Tia!

            They drink.

TIA: Thanks, guys.

            She and STEVE kiss.

ROBIN: Are you going to do long distance?

STEVE: I'm going with her. The timing seems right.

TIA: And I wrote a part for him.

ROBIN: I'd love to read it.

STEVE: Why don't we read it now?

TIA: Really?

PATRICIA: I'm game.

STEVE: We can huddle round your laptop.

TIA: Robin, do you want to?

ROBIN: Sure, I'd love to forget where I am for a while.

TIA: Great! You can be Princess Elizabeth.

ROBIN: (*As ELIZABETH.*) It would be my honour.

TIA: Patricia, you'll be Mercy. I'll be Faith.

STEVE: And I'm the dashing Montague.

TIA: Wait, who will play Talbot?

PATRICIA: Who's that?

TIA: Elizabeth's envoy.

ROBIN: Let's take turns being the white guy.

TIA: Good plan. (*Reading.*) *Comportment Lessons for Serving the Future Queen* by Tia Mwangi.

            PATRICIA and ROBIN vocalize their doubt.

            What?

ROBIN: A tad long.

TIA: It's a working title.

ROBIN: Good.

TIA: (*Reading from her laptop.*) Act one, scene one. It is January nineteen fifty-two. The setting is a small restaurant in Nyeri, Kenya. A mother and daughter are taking down Christmas decorations.

                        THE END